What's Really in the Big Beautiful Bill

Decoding 900 Pages That Will Redefine Your Life

SOUTHERLAND | COPYRIGHT 2025

Chapter 1: The Beast Unveiled   5

Chapter 2: SNAP Overhaul – New Caps, Fewer Deductions 9

Chapter 3: SNAP Work Wrangle   13

Chapter 4: State Stakes in SNAP   18

Chapter 5: SNAP Nutrition Education Ends   22

Chapter 6: Immigrant Access to SNAP Tightened   25

Chapter 7: Medicaid Eligibility Freeze   29

Chapter 8: Medicaid Cleanup Measures   34

Chapter 9: Medicaid Payment Penalties   37

Chapter 10: Medicaid Asset Test Tightened   42

Chapter 11: Immigrant and Emergency Medicaid Limits   46

Chapter 12: Long-Term Care Staffing Freeze   49

Chapter 13: Reduced Provider Incentives   53

Chapter 14: Budget-Neutral Pilot Projects Only   56

Chapter 15: Medicaid Work and Cost-Sharing Rules   58

Chapter 16: Green Energy Rollbacks and Fossil Fuel
Favoritism   62

Chapter 17: Student Loans, Education, and Borrowing Limits
67

Chapter 18: Immigration, Border, and Asylum Enforcement Changes
71

Chapter 19: Legal Enforcement and Implementation Mechanics
75

Chapter 20: Tax Benefits Phasing & Limits Remaining   79

Chapter 21: Clean Energy Credit Rollbacks   84

Chapter 22: Carbon Capture & Clean-Tech Cuts   88

Chapter 23: Clean-Fossil Hybrid Incentives   93

Chapter 24: Education & Student Loan Overhaul   97

Chapter 25: Immigration & Border Enforcement   101

Chapter 26: Detention and Asylum Work Limits   105

Chapter 27: Implementation Timelines & Sunset Clauses 110

Chapter 28: Restricted Agency Flexibility   113

Chapter 29: Legal Bond Barrier   117

Chapter 30: Longevity by Legal Rigidity   121

Chapter 31: Everyday Impact Snapshot   124

Chapter 32: Winners, Losers, and Trade-Offs   130

Chapter 33: Equity and Access Concerns   134

Chapter 34: Legislative Game Plan   138

Chapter 35: Restricted Agency Flexibility   142

Chapter 36: Legal Bond Barrier   146

Chapter 37: Longevity by Legal Rigidity   149

Chapter 38: Everyday Impact Snapshot   153

Chapter 39: Winners, Losers, and Trade-Offs   157

Chapter 40: Equity and Access Concerns   160

Chapter 1: The Beast Unveiled

Let's not waste time pretending this is just another routine legislative package. It's not. This is a 900-page bureaucratic monolith with enough embedded policy landmines to alter the ground beneath nearly every working- and middle-class American—and plenty of upper-middle types too smug to notice they're next. It's not clever. It's not efficient. It's the product of political cowardice and economic sleight-of-hand posing as reform. If you're looking for integrity, you came to the wrong bill.

You probably heard it pitched as "relief." They always do that. Tax relief. Healthcare reform. A pro-family agenda. If a law needs a PR campaign, it's usually bad news wearing a smile. This one's no exception. It slaps together tax breaks, benefit clawbacks, work requirements, and regulatory shivs under the pretense of fairness, responsibility, and—God help us— "modernization." But strip away the branding, and what you're left with is a cynical rearrangement of burdens dressed up as bipartisan pragmatism.

It doesn't fix broken systems. It rearranges them to hurt different people.

Let's get this straight from the top: the bill is too long, intentionally. When Congress writes a 900-page Frankenstein stitched from dozens of separate committee drafts, they're not trying to communicate. They're hiding things. This is the legislative equivalent of burying the murder weapon under a landfill of footnotes and cross-references. And the people who vote for it? Most of them haven't read past the summary their staff emailed them two hours before the floor vote.

So what's really in it? Start with the structure: tax law rewrites, social program eligibility restrictions, funding reallocations, and enforcement mechanisms designed less to solve problems than to establish control. This bill isn't designed to improve your life. It's designed to make sure any improvement stays within a rigid, state-controlled budget box, while the upper class dodges accountability and the lower class gets a new set of hoops to jump through.

The bill locks in frozen food benefit benchmarks for SNAP, strips away access to Medicaid through hyper-aggressive eligibility policing, and slashes clean energy subsidies while boosting fossil fuel incentives. But the real trick is how it sells these guttings as fiscal discipline. Discipline for whom? Not the oil companies getting new deductions. Not the defense contractors whose budget line items remain untouched. No, the "discipline" falls—as always—on the people without lobbyists or campaign cash: the gig workers, the caretakers, the retirees who still file because they can't afford not to.

And here's the part too many people miss: this isn't reform. It's containment. It's about locking economic mobility into a narrow corridor—offering just enough to keep people quiet, but never enough to give them leverage. The tax changes? Structured to benefit people already filing. Already stable. Already in the system. If you're below the line, you get nothing but more bureaucracy and another damn deadline.

This is not just policy by spreadsheet. It's policy by spreadsheet held hostage by political optics. Congress needed to look like it was doing something big. So it did. And it made sure that "big" didn't threaten anyone with real power. The Medicaid reforms? Designed to make budget projections prettier, not care delivery better. The student loan limits? Pitched as cost control, when they're really a backdoor subsidy to private lenders. The Trump Account? A glorified $1,000 savings bond they'll pretend changes lives. Newsflash: it won't. Not without systemic follow-through, and this bill provides none.

Even the timeline is rigged. Most major provisions don't kick in until 2026. Why? Because that gives the current crop of lawmakers time to ride the headline buzz, campaign off the "reforms," and leave the implementation to some poor sucker down the line. It's a legislative game of hot potato. But the people who get burned won't be in office—they'll be sitting at their kitchen tables wondering why their tax credit disappeared and their Medicaid renewal got rejected for missing paperwork they never got.

And don't get distracted by the headlines. "No tax on tips." "Overtime relief." "New baby savings accounts." These are bait. They sound bold, but they're built on income thresholds, phaseouts, and fine print that neutralize their impact. If you qualify, great—enjoy your extra few hundred bucks. But most people won't. That's the point. The real game is the money saved by denying access.

The bill also expands state accountability. Which sounds good, until you realize what that means: pressure. States are punished for administrative errors, overpayments, and lax enforcement. So what do they do? They clamp down. They delay processing. They make it harder to apply. They audit more aggressively.

Not because it's just, but because it's required. The feds outsource the cruelty, then claim their hands are clean.

There's nothing inherently wrong with oversight or spending limits. But when the cuts land on food, healthcare, education, and energy relief while leaving corporate loopholes intact, we're not talking about balance. We're talking about class warfare masquerading as fiscal stewardship.

And buried deeper still are the legal entrenchments—clauses that block agencies from softening enforcement, even during emergencies. Courts can't grant relief unless you pay a bond, a literal price tag on due process. That's not policy. That's preemptive authoritarianism written into administrative law.

Let's not pretend this happened by accident. This is not a flawed bill with good intentions. This is a blueprint, carefully drafted, ruthlessly layered, and deliberately opaque. It's a structural bet against upward mobility, against transparency, and against the idea that government should serve people instead of managing them.

So welcome to the "big beautiful bill." It's neither big for the right reasons, nor beautiful in any meaningful sense of the word. But it is a bill. And like every bill crafted by a coalition of technocrats, ideologues, and political survivors, it's about power first, policy second, and the public dead last.

You want to know what's coming? Read it. Understand it. Because what's coming isn't help. It's compliance. It's conditions. It's cost-sharing, means-testing, and another set of hoops just high enough to make sure the wrong people can't reach them.

This isn't governance. It's management by attrition. And if you think this is where it ends, you haven't been paying attention.

Chapter 2: SNAP Overhaul – New Caps, Fewer Deductions

This chapter of the bill doesn't just tweak the Supplemental Nutrition Assistance Program—it surgically constricts it. Anyone claiming this is a "modernization" of food benefits either hasn't read the fine print or is lying through their teeth. This isn't a diet for the federal budget—it's a starvation protocol for the poor.

Let's start with the freeze. The government's beloved Thrifty Food Plan—the benchmark they use to determine how much help families get—has been effectively put in a cryogenic state. No more updates based on actual dietary science or evolving nutritional standards. It's locked down until 2027. Even then, it can't be changed unless the USDA performs a full-scale re-evaluation that explicitly doesn't raise overall costs. That's right: even if food prices soar or dietary needs evolve, the benefit amounts can't follow unless it fits within a budget cap designed by people who wouldn't know what a SNAP application looks like if it slapped them in the face.

Translation: benefits will stagnate, nutritional needs will be ignored, and recipients will get stuck with outdated baselines that pretend inflation doesn't affect groceries.

And what about family size? The maximum benefit amount caps out at 200% of a four-person household's allotment. If you've got eight or more mouths to feed, tough luck. After that point, you're punished for existing. This cap doesn't adjust for economies of scale or regional cost differences. It's one-size-fits-nobody.

Now let's talk about work requirements—the shiny object waved around by politicians who think poverty is a motivational issue. Under the new rules, anyone between 18 and 65 who isn't working at least 80 hours per month, or enrolled in approved training, risks losing their benefits. This assumes jobs are plentiful, transportation is easy, and every adult has the mental and physical capacity to jump through hoops on demand. Spoiler: they don't.

There are carveouts, of course. If you're pregnant, disabled, caring for a child under 14, or part of a federally recognized tribe, you're exempt. But here's the catch: the exemptions still rely on documentation, state-level processing, and bureaucratic consistency—three things SNAP is rarely blessed with. And the enforcement? Much harsher now. States have to prove they're cracking down, with quarterly progress reports and performance metrics. Fall short, and the feds cut your funding.

This creates exactly the kind of perverse incentive that punishes administrators for erring on the side of compassion. Instead, they're nudged to preemptively deny, delay, and disqualify. Not because they want to, but because the algorithm of funding survival demands it.

Alaska and Hawaii get a temporary reprieve on waivers, but only if they jump through their own set of hoops. They must demonstrate "good faith compliance"—whatever that means—and their exemptions expire by 2028. The rest of the states? Left to navigate this increasingly hostile administrative jungle with fewer tools and more risk.

And if that weren't enough, the bill takes a hacksaw to how utility expenses factor into SNAP calculations. Until now, households that received energy assistance got a higher shelter deduction, which helped them qualify for more food support. Logical, right? If you spend more on heat, you have less for groceries. But not anymore. Going forward, unless your household includes an elderly or disabled member, you lose that deduction.

Oh, and internet expenses? Deleted. Erased. Irrelevant. Never mind that internet access is essential for job applications, remote work, school assignments, and accessing the very benefit portals the government wants you to use. In the eyes of this bill, broadband is a luxury—not a necessity. So when they calculate how much help you deserve, your $60 monthly internet bill might as well be spent on champagne and cigars.

Now let's turn to state accountability, the latest euphemism for bureaucratic punishment. States are now financially penalized if their SNAP error rate exceeds 10%. Go above the threshold and lose 15% of your federal funding. Fall somewhere in the middle and you still get docked. The result? State agencies are given every incentive to err on the side of denial, tighten eligibility screening, and prioritize "accuracy" over access.

And who decides what counts as an error? Not the people applying. Not the caseworkers trying to manage bloated caseloads. No, the feds. From afar. With spreadsheets. It's policy enforcement without proximity—cold, mechanical, and deeply flawed.

As if that weren't enough, the federal government is yanking back its share of administrative costs. Historically, USDA covered 50% of what it cost states to run SNAP. Starting in 2027, that drops to 25%. That means states have to cough up the other 75% just to maintain the same level of service. With what budget, exactly? That's not the federal government's problem anymore.

Expect layoffs, application backlogs, longer wait times, and fewer staff. All of this happening while the pressure to verify, cross-check, and deny benefits is ramping up. It's a bureaucratic death spiral engineered by people who've never stood in a benefits office line in their lives.

Now, let's talk about public health—specifically, the part they're cutting. The National Education and Obesity Prevention Program, which funded community classes on healthy eating, budgeting, and diabetes prevention, gets terminated in 2025. Because why invest in education when you can just penalize people for failing a test no one helped them study for?

And finally, we arrive at immigration. Only U.S. citizens, lawful permanent residents, a narrow band of Cuban and Haitian entrants, and a few COFA (Compact of Free Association) nationals are still eligible for SNAP. Everyone else, including legal non-citizens with temporary or indeterminate status, is out.

But here's the kicker: even if someone in your household isn't eligible, their income still counts when determining your benefit. So if you've got a mixed-status family—legal, working, paying taxes—you can get hit with reduced benefits simply because one member doesn't have the right paperwork.

This isn't an accident. It's a design feature. The bill weaponizes eligibility math to punish mixed-status families by stealth. They're not denied outright—they're just squeezed until they fall off the rolls by default.

So to recap: the government is freezing benefits against inflation, capping household size penalties, tightening work requirements, removing shelter deductions, punishing states for administrative error, cutting public health education, slashing cost-sharing, and narrowing immigration eligibility. All while pretending this is somehow "targeted reform."

It's not reform. It's retribution with a spreadsheet.

SNAP used to be a lifeline. Now it's a conditional favor. A ration card with strings attached. And those strings? They're tightening.

Chapter 3: SNAP Work Wrangle

Let's kill the illusion right here: work requirements don't increase employment. They reduce benefits. That's the point. Anyone who tells you this provision is about lifting people up has either never opened a policy impact report or is just parroting talking points from a staffer who skimmed one. This isn't about jobs. It's about punishment with paperwork.

The new work requirements target so-called "able-bodied adults without dependents" between the ages of 18 and 65. It's a neat bureaucratic term that treats millions of Americans as if they were dead weight until proven otherwise. Under the new rule, if you're not working at least 80 hours a month—or in an "approved" training program—you're out. That's not a suggestion. That's a cliff. No job, no benefits.

On paper, this sounds fair to people who think the job market is a buffet of opportunity and not a revolving door of temp gigs, zero-hour contracts, and "we'll call you back." But in reality, it penalizes the exact population most affected by labor instability: part-time workers, gig workers, and people in rural or high-unemployment regions where jobs don't grow on trees—they evaporate.

The bill makes a big show of exemptions, as if to soften the blow. Pregnant? Exempt. Medically unfit for work? Exempt. Caring for a child under 14? Sure. Over 65? You're off the hook. Members of federally recognized tribes or urban Indians? Also excluded. These carveouts are fine in theory. But they rely on one thing: bureaucratic proof. And if you think verification is clean, timely, or accurate, you've clearly never navigated the SNAP bureaucracy while juggling a life on the edge.

Here's what "enforcement" now looks like: more documentation, more frequent check-ins, and a narrower margin for error. One missed deadline. One unsigned form. One job that doesn't meet the right definition of "work"—and you're done. No food. No appeal worth the wait. Just a cold termination letter written in legalese that blames you for failing a system you were never equipped to win.

And the states? Oh, they're under the gun too. Waivers that used to allow for local flexibility—pausing work requirements during recessions or in hard-hit counties—are now nearly impossible to get. States must prove "extraordinary circumstances" just to apply. And even if they do qualify, the waiver comes with strings: quarterly compliance reports, benchmarks, and expiration dates that guarantee no long-term relief. This isn't local control. It's federal extortion with a smiling face.

The only two states with some breathing room are Alaska and Hawaii. They can still apply for waivers through 2028, but only if they're demonstrating "good faith efforts" to meet federal targets. It's a conditional reprieve, not a gift. And when 2028 hits? They're back under the same thumb as everyone else.

Let's pause for a reality check. People who need SNAP often work. They work in jobs without benefits, without stable hours, and with bosses who think scheduling is a game of roulette. Requiring 80 hours a month doesn't sound like much until you remember those hours have to be consistent, trackable, and verifiable. Good luck getting that from Uber, TaskRabbit, or the third under-the-table job you took to pay rent.

And let's not forget that training programs—the supposed alternative—are limited, waitlisted, and regionally inconsistent. Being "in training" sounds good until the program you qualify for starts three months from now, or requires transportation you don't have. Then what? You don't meet the rule, and SNAP shuts you out.

This is the heart of the con: creating requirements that sound fair but are functionally designed to fail. The goal isn't to help people work. The goal is to reduce enrollment numbers and call it success. That's how "savings" are scored. Not by improving outcomes, but by lowering participation through forced attrition.

And don't expect consistency. States vary wildly in how they track, verify, and enforce work requirements. Some have sophisticated databases. Others rely on error-prone manual reviews. Many subcontract to third parties—vendors who are incentivized to close cases, not open them. So even if you meet the 80-hour rule, it's entirely possible the system won't recognize it. Then it's your fault for "non-compliance." Not the system's fault for being broken.

The new quarterly reports required from states add another layer of pressure. Miss your performance targets? Funding gets slashed. Welcome to the audit economy, where public benefits are managed like risk portfolios and recipients are treated like liabilities.

This has already played out before. States that implemented strict work requirements in the past saw no long-term employment boost. What they saw was disenrollment. Food insecurity went up. Compliance errors skyrocketed. And the administrative costs of enforcing these rules often exceeded the savings from cutting people off. But who cares about data when the politics of punishment poll better?

And of course, this all happens while the feds cut their share of administrative support. So states are expected to do more with less: more reporting, more enforcement, more oversight—with half the resources they used to have. That's not policy improvement. That's sabotage through budget starvation.

Let's also consider who this hits hardest. It's not the truly destitute, who may still qualify under other rules. It's the precarious: the single adult trying to string together 20 hours a week from three part-time gigs. The person in recovery who just got back into the workforce. The caretaker whose hours fluctuate based on someone else's hospital schedule. These people get caught in the gears and blamed for "non-compliance."

And what happens when they fall off SNAP? They don't magically become self-sufficient. They get hungrier. They skip meals. They lean harder on already-fractured local food banks and charities. And guess what? Hungry people don't job-hunt well. They don't train well. They don't get healthier. They just get quieter, weaker, and more desperate.

If this were really about promoting work, it would invest in job placement, transit access, and career training. It doesn't. If it were about accountability, it would hold employers responsible for unstable hours and illegal underpayment. It doesn't. If it were about helping people move forward, it wouldn't cut them off for failing to jump through burning bureaucratic hoops. But it does.

Because this isn't about outcomes. It's about optics. Reducing the number of SNAP recipients makes for a good soundbite, even if it makes for a lousy society. And as long as lawmakers can frame that drop as "success," they'll keep pulling the same lever, no matter how many people it crushes.

Welcome to the SNAP work wrangle. Where effort doesn't matter, paperwork is weaponized, and survival is conditional. Again.

Chapter 4: State Stakes in SNAP

This chapter doesn't play around. It's where the federal government hands the guillotine to the states and tells them to manage their food assistance programs with "precision"—or else. The result? A bureaucratic game of chicken where the poor are the ones sent flying off the cliff.

Let's talk about error rates. The bill introduces a new performance metric that's both vague and vicious: if your state's SNAP error rate is under 6%, congratulations, you keep full federal support. Slip between 6% and 10%? Your funding gets docked. Blow past 10%? You lose 15% of your federal matching funds for those payments. The logic? A high error rate must mean waste or fraud. The reality? Most of the time, it means the forms were filled out wrong, a clerical glitch triggered a false flag, or someone didn't return paperwork they never received.

But nuance doesn't fund congressional campaign ads. So, they wrote in punitive thresholds and called it efficiency.

Here's the math states are now forced to do: spend more on verification, staff, oversight, and data compliance to keep error rates low—or risk losing millions in federal funds. And if they don't have that budget flexibility (and most don't), they'll just tighten the front-end of the application process. More documentation. More denials. Longer wait times. Less human judgment. It's administrative triage, with the safety net as the casualty.

Think that's an exaggeration? Go ask any state-level SNAP administrator how much bandwidth they have to process cases accurately and quickly when their budget gets slashed mid-year. The answer is always some combination of "we can't" and "we'll try." And now they're being told to hit precision marks that even Fortune 500 payroll systems don't consistently hit.

And that's just the beginning. The federal administrative cost-sharing structure—the backbone of how states run these programs—is getting cut in half. It used to be a 50/50 match. Starting in 2027, it's 75/25, with the feds paying just a quarter. That's a forced cost shift of billions over time, dumped on state budgets that are already bleeding from healthcare, education, and public safety shortfalls.

Where's that money supposed to come from? Not from cutting checks to overpaid consultants or pet infrastructure projects, apparently. No, the easiest place to find "efficiencies" is in the SNAP program itself. Fewer caseworkers. Fewer outreach staff. Fewer eligibility assistants. Which, predictably, leads to more mistakes—exactly the thing that triggers penalties in the first place.

You see the loop? Underfunded programs create more errors. More errors trigger funding cuts. Cuts lead to more underfunding. Rinse, repeat, collapse.

Now throw automation into the mix. Many states already rely on brittle legacy systems to process benefits. They were built in the early 2000s, patched during the Great Recession, and duct-taped during COVID. The idea that these creaky systems can handle higher verification standards, real-time income checks, and intricate utility deductions while also reducing errors is fantasy bordering on malicious optimism. But Congress doesn't care. They passed the mandate and walked away.

So what do states do? They outsource. Enter the private sector—contractors who promise slick interfaces and AI-driven verification tools that supposedly streamline the application process. They rarely do. What they actually deliver is a polished denial machine. One that flags inconsistencies without context and punts appeals to overworked staff who no longer have time for case-by-case reviews.

And here's where it gets dangerous: states are incentivized to close cases quickly, not accurately. Better to deny up front than risk an error that triggers a funding penalty later. That's not paranoia—it's risk management under duress. If you're a state director facing budget pressure, do you err on the side of generosity or on the side of job security?

The pressure flows downhill. Caseworkers are told to hit quotas, reduce backlog, and eliminate ambiguities. Translation: treat every applicant like a suspect until they prove otherwise. The result? People get denied not because they don't qualify, but because their lives don't fit into the spreadsheet-approved format the system requires.

That's especially brutal for workers with volatile incomes—Uber drivers, seasonal employees, caretakers, and people paid under-the-table out of necessity, not choice. The system doesn't like their paperwork, so it throws them out. And when they appeal, the wait times stretch from weeks to months. In the meantime, they starve—or borrow—or both.

Meanwhile, states are still expected to improve access, reduce food insecurity, and meet the rising need caused by inflation and wage stagnation. But they have to do it with less money, less staff, more rules, and the looming threat of federal punishment if they screw it up.

So they play it safe. Not safe for the public—safe for the budget. Applications get slower. Approvals get tighter. Outreach programs dry up. The message is clear: if you need help, good luck navigating the labyrinth. And if you get lost, it's your fault.

This chapter doesn't reform state SNAP programs. It destabilizes them. It turns state agencies into compliance labs, not service providers. The poor become data points, the programs become performance metrics, and the people running them are turned into crisis managers.

And it's only going to get worse.

Because the goal isn't just to reduce fraud or improve outcomes. It's to shrink the number of people receiving benefits. Not because their lives improved—but because the application process got too hostile, the staffing got too thin, or the funding got cut one too many times.

This is what happens when lawmakers use metrics to avoid responsibility. They set benchmarks that look good on a graph and then blame the states when the system crashes under the weight of those expectations.

The federal government wrote a check with this chapter, but it's the states who have to cash it—with overdraft fees. And the people who rely on these benefits? They're just another liability to manage, not a need to meet.

Welcome to the new SNAP reality: where success is measured in denials, and failure looks a lot like being hungry in a country that says it can't afford to feed you—but somehow never runs out of money for war, bailouts, or tax shelters.

Chapter 5: SNAP Nutrition Education Ends

This is the part they hope you won't notice—because it's not flashy, it doesn't involve a tax credit, and nobody's filming campaign ads in front of a crumbling community center. But this is where the knife goes in quietly. The bill ends funding for one of the most unglamorous, yet effective, pieces of the SNAP ecosystem: the nutrition education and obesity prevention program. You probably never heard about it. That's because it actually worked.

Officially called SNAP-Ed, this program funded community-level initiatives to teach people how to stretch their benefits without sacrificing nutrition. We're talking about cooking classes, grocery store walk-throughs, budget meal planning, diabetes prevention workshops—real, practical education. Not lectures. Not shaming. Just skills.

In other words, it did what every politician claims to support: it gave people tools, not just handouts. But now it's gone. Not trimmed. Not reevaluated. Eliminated. Finished after 2025. No hearings. No headlines. Just a quiet burial in the middle of a 900-page legislative corpse.

And the justification? Budget constraints, of course. Because apparently, a few million a year helping people eat better is where we draw the fiscal line—right after writing in new deductions for oil companies and deferring taxes on private jets. If you think this cut is about saving money, I have a surplus Pentagon procurement report to sell you.

Here's what this actually kills: outreach workers in food deserts showing people how to buy a week's worth of meals without blowing half their benefits on processed garbage. Partnerships with schools and local health departments teaching kids the difference between real food and sugar-laced trash. Programs helping diabetics avoid amputations by adjusting their diet instead of increasing their insulin dosage. But sure, let's call that "non-essential."

You want to know what's going to replace these programs? Nothing. Not a damn thing. There is no federal backfill, no state block grant, no local mandate to step in. These were community-driven efforts, funded precisely because market forces and state budgets don't support them. You don't make a profit teaching a single mom how to cook lentils. But you sure as hell reduce Medicaid costs down the line. Too bad this bill doesn't do nuance—it does cuts.

And let's talk about who loses. Not the affluent urbanite who can afford a CSA box and a nutritionist. Not the boomer filing from his suburban retirement community with a well-stocked fridge and Medicare on tap. No, this hits the low-income family in a rural zip code where the grocery store is a gas station and the vegetables are canned, if they exist at all. It hits the senior living on $1,200 a month trying to avoid congestive heart failure with a budget of $4 per day. It hits kids growing up on boxed food and soda because no one ever taught them what "fiber" even is.

This was one of the rare programs that saw the poor as capable and deserving of investment. It didn't talk down to them. It didn't test them. It didn't punish them for being poor. It gave them information, access, and some dignity. And for that, it had to go.

If you think this is hyperbole, go read the internal evaluations. SNAP-Ed had measurable impact—better food choices, lower obesity rates, fewer ER visits related to diet. Not dramatic, not overnight, but steady, consistent, and cost-effective. In policy terms, it was a rare thing: small dollars, big returns. Which, naturally, made it a target.

Why? Because helping people succeed makes it harder to justify future cuts. It ruins the narrative. You can't say "the system is broken" while actively defunding the parts that work. You can't sell the lie that poor people don't care about their health if they've got access to classes proving otherwise. SNAP-Ed was inconvenient proof that education and empowerment matter. And the last thing this bill wants is inconvenient proof.

So, it was axed. Not with malice—malice requires intention. This was worse. This was indifference. This was Congress looking at a line item marked "nutrition outreach" and saying, "No one votes on that." They were right. No one did. And now we all get to pay the price.

Because here's the truth: when people lose access to nutrition education, they don't stop eating. They eat worse. They get sicker. They develop chronic conditions earlier and die younger. Their healthcare costs rise. Their children carry the same habits into adulthood. This is how generational poverty works—through small decisions with large consequences.

But hey, someone's tax bracket just got protected. Someone's PAC just wrote a thank-you check. Someone's cable news appearance got a talking point about cutting "waste." And the rest of us? We get to explain to the next wave of diabetic 30-year-olds why their SNAP card doesn't come with the education their parents used to get.

This cut is cynical. It's cowardly. And it's exactly what you get when legislation is written not to solve problems, but to preserve power. Nutrition education isn't a handout. It's infrastructure. And we just demolished it without blinking.

Welcome to the brave new world of SNAP. You can still get some calories, sure—if you qualify. But don't expect any help figuring out what to do with them. That's on you now. And if it goes wrong, don't worry. They'll blame you too.

Chapter 6: Immigrant Access to SNAP Tightened

Let's dispense with the usual sanctimonious garbage right away: this chapter isn't about "protecting benefits for citizens" or "ensuring integrity in the system." It's about targeting immigrants—plain and simple. And not just undocumented immigrants, which is the red meat line thrown to the press corps. This bill carves into legal immigrants. People who followed the rules. Paid taxes. Contributed. Still excluded.

The language is surgical. Only U.S. citizens, lawful permanent residents (green card holders), a narrow group of Cuban and Haitian entrants, and those residing under a Compact of Free Association agreement can now receive SNAP benefits. Everyone else? Out. Doesn't matter if they've worked here for years. Doesn't matter if they're paying into the system. Doesn't matter if they're waiting on a bureaucratic backlog they didn't create. If their papers aren't just right, the system shuts the door.

But here's where it gets really cynical. Even if someone is disqualified, their income still counts against the household. So if you're a mixed-status family—say, a U.S. citizen child with two undocumented parents—the system pretends you have more income than you do. The ineligible adult can't receive food benefits, but their income is still used to reduce the child's allotment. It's punitive accounting. The equivalent of taxing someone on money they don't actually get to spend.

This isn't a loophole. It's designed. It's a silent punishment for proximity to the "wrong" kind of immigrant. Doesn't matter if your spouse is a tax-paying, working resident. If their visa isn't one of the blessed few, you and your citizen kids will eat less. That's not an accident. It's a deterrent strategy dressed up as eligibility reform.

And no, this isn't about fraud. Fraud rates in SNAP are already laughably low—under 1.5%, and most of that is transactional error, not criminal conspiracy. Immigrant households are more likely to be food insecure than fraudulent. But punishing them plays well in headlines. It makes lawmakers look "tough" without actually having to do the hard work of improving the system.

This is where economic policy meets culture war. The people who wrote this section know damn well who's affected. Legal immigrants stuck in the backlog. Families where only some members are citizens. Refugees with temporary status. DACA recipients living in limbo. These aren't criminals. They're not drains. They're working people who fall into the gray zone between political expedience and actual fairness.

And let's not pretend this happens in a vacuum. These same families are being squeezed on all sides—rising rents, stagnant wages, healthcare exclusions, childcare barriers—and now the food assistance floor is being pulled out from under them. That's not reform. That's sabotage.

You want to guess who this hits hardest? Women. Children. Elderly immigrants. The same demographics who already carry disproportionate burdens in healthcare, labor, and housing. But sure, let's cut their food assistance because a Senate subcommittee thinks "eligibility enforcement" polls better than "basic decency."

This isn't just about numbers. It's about signal. The message being sent is clear: even if you're legal, even if you're working, even if your kids were born here—you are not welcome at the safety net. The bill doesn't say it outright, but the math does. And families feel it in the groceries they can't buy and the benefits they don't receive.

What's particularly galling is how this restriction will be enforced. Not by ICE. Not by raids. But by caseworkers staring at computer screens trying to decode complex immigration codes and eligibility trees built by people who never had to navigate them. Mistakes will be made. Eligibility will be misjudged. And appeals will take months, if they even happen. In the meantime, kids go hungry. Parents skip meals. And bureaucrats meet performance metrics that look clean but reek of systemic cruelty.

This is the same old game, played with newer tools. Cut benefits, frame the cut as fairness, and let the fallout fall hardest on those with the least voice. Immigrant communities already live with legal precarity. Now we're adding nutritional precarity to the mix. Because nothing says "American values" like feeding some kids and starving others based on what their parents' paperwork looks like.

And just to be clear: this will not save significant money. The immigrant population excluded by this provision is a tiny fraction of overall SNAP recipients. The cost of enforcing it— training caseworkers, updating eligibility software, fielding appeals, managing errors—will probably exceed the savings. But it will allow lawmakers to say they "tightened the rules." And in an election cycle, that's worth more than food on anyone's table.

Let's be blunt: this is policy by scapegoating. It exploits the myth that immigrants are somehow leeching off the system, while quietly subsidizing corporate agriculture, underpaying migrant labor, and ignoring the billions in taxes paid by people who will never see a dime in return. It is hypocritical, performative, and cowardly.

If you want to reduce food insecurity, you expand access. You don't ration it with a litmus test of legal purity. But this bill isn't about reducing hunger. It's about tightening control—on spending, on people, and on who gets to be seen as "deserving."

Immigrants, as usual, are excluded from that category. Not because it makes policy sense, but because it makes political theater.

So let's not pretend this section is an oversight. It's a feature. A feature built on fear, marketed as discipline, and enforced through silence. And when the grocery carts get lighter and the food pantries get fuller, don't say you didn't know. It's all written right here—in plain English, buried under 900 pages of legislative misdirection.

Chapter 7: Medicaid Eligibility Freeze

If you've spent any time navigating the Medicaid system—or watching someone try to—you already know it's less a healthcare program and more an administrative endurance test. This chapter takes that rigged obstacle course and cements it in concrete. No shortcuts. No flexibility. Just new rules written by people who have never filled out an eligibility redetermination form in their lives.

Let's begin with what the bill *stopped*. Two federal rules were on deck to expand Medicaid access—one designed to boost enrollment in Medicare Savings Programs (for low-income seniors), the other aimed at simplifying applications for Medicaid, CHIP, and the Basic Health Program. Together, they were poised to streamline eligibility across programs that often overlap in the real world but operate like rival corporations behind the scenes.

Those rules? Now frozen. Not revised, not refined—just indefinitely blocked. Because why let poor seniors enroll more easily in programs that keep them from rationing medication when you can instead protect the sacred budget scorecard from the horror of more people actually getting care?

This isn't a delay to fix bugs. It's a stall to avoid enrollment increases. These were administrative tweaks, not massive new entitlements. But even minor expansions threaten the fiction that Medicaid is "too generous." So the bill slams the brakes and pretends that's responsibility, not cowardice.

But the freeze is just the appetizer. The main course is a sweeping mandate to reduce "duplicate enrollment" between Medicaid and CHIP. On paper, this sounds like eliminating waste. In practice, it means more red tape for families whose kids might be on CHIP while parents are on Medicaid. If your state's IT systems don't talk to each other—and most don't—you could get booted from one program while trying to stay enrolled in the other.

And it gets better. The bill now requires states to regularly audit Medicaid rolls to remove the deceased. Sounds reasonable. Until you realize that many states still rely on outdated death records, flawed matching algorithms, and slow interagency reporting. The outcome? Live people get purged. Real patients get treated like database errors.

Same story for deceased providers. Clinics that closed or doctors who passed away may still be billing through lagging systems. So the bill mandates state cleanup. Again, not a bad goal—but completely unfunded. The burden of updating, verifying, and cross-checking this data in real time falls squarely on state agencies already running on fumes.

Here's where the hammer drops. If states are found to be making "excess payments"—a term loosely defined and generously applied—the federal government will reduce its matching funds. In other words: find a mistake, cut their funding. The message? Clean up your books or pay the price.

Now think about how that plays out. Understaffed agencies will start flagging anything remotely suspect. Payment delays. Coverage terminations. Appeals left unanswered. The system chokes itself trying to be "accurate" and ends up being vindictive.

And this isn't theoretical. Every state with a bloated, error-prone Medicaid IT system just got handed a loaded gun and told to enforce perfection. Meanwhile, enrollees—the people actually needing care—get caught in the gears. One missed form, one mismatched record, one month of slightly higher income, and you're out.

Which brings us to redeterminations. The bill mandates that states check Medicaid eligibility more frequently. It doesn't say how often—it leaves that to the feds to decide later—but the intent is clear: check more, deny more. Anyone with fluctuating income—seasonal workers, gig workers, hourly staff with inconsistent hours—gets hit hardest.

These are the people who often qualify one month and miss the cutoff the next, through no fault of their own. But under this new regime, they'll be churned in and out of coverage like defective products on a conveyor belt. Not because their needs changed, but because their paperwork didn't match last week's paycheck stub.

And then there's the home equity rule. Medicaid already restricts long-term care eligibility based on how much your home is worth. This bill tightens that further. Yes, it raises the maximum value threshold in theory, but it also allows states to set their own, lower caps. So seniors in modest homes could find themselves disqualified from the very care they spent a lifetime paying taxes to receive.

The result? Elderly homeowners face a brutal choice: sell the house or give up care. This isn't theoretical. It's already happening in states with aggressive asset tests. Now the federal government is giving every state permission to follow suit— and even cheering them on.

And let's not forget immigration. The bill restricts Medicaid access to lawful residents only. Emergency Medicaid still exists, but routine care? Gone for anyone without pristine legal status. That includes people in mixed-status families, DACA recipients, and immigrants in process. It's the same playbook as the SNAP restrictions: frame it as integrity, use it as exclusion.

This chapter also suspends federal staffing mandates for long-term care facilities. These rules were meant to improve nurse-to-patient ratios in nursing homes—a response to the carnage we saw during COVID. But now they're on hold. Facilities can run lean, cut corners, and save money. The trade-off? Lower quality care, more preventable deaths, and a system that treats elderly bodies as budget liabilities.

The broader mandate here is unmistakable: reduce Medicaid spending at all costs. The bill tells states to trim eligibility, lower reimbursement rates, and eliminate services that go beyond federal minimums. Translation: cover fewer people, offer fewer benefits, and pray the lawsuits take a few years to land.

And speaking of lawsuits, the bill puts a pause on any significant demonstration projects unless they're budget-neutral from the start. Innovation is now a liability. If a state wants to pilot a new model for care—telehealth expansion, integrated care systems, or preventive wellness—they have to prove in advance that it won't cost a dime more. That kills experimentation. That kills progress.

This chapter doesn't fix Medicaid. It fortifies it—against the poor, the sick, and the working class. It's a firewall of red tape, asset testing, eligibility churn, and state-level administrative terror. All wrapped in the language of "integrity" and "cost control," while the actual goal is containment, exclusion, and eventual attrition.

And don't be fooled by the slow rollout. The phase-ins are staggered over years, not because they're complex, but because delay gives cover. It buys time for lawmakers to dodge responsibility. By the time the hammer actually falls, the people who wrote this poison will be long gone—raking in private-sector checks while Medicaid directors are left holding the bag.

This isn't policy. It's malpractice with a legislative memo attached. And if you're relying on Medicaid—or know someone who is—you better start reading the fine print now. Because the safety net is being redrawn with thinner lines and wider holes.

And this time, falling through won't be an accident. It's the plan.

Chapter 8: Medicaid Cleanup Measures

Let's start with the dead people. Yes, the bill mandates that states remove deceased beneficiaries from Medicaid rolls. In theory, a no-brainer. Of course dead people shouldn't be receiving benefits. But here's the real-world problem: the death data is garbage.

Many state systems still operate on outdated or disconnected databases. Deaths reported in one system don't automatically update in another. Hospitals notify one agency. The Social Security Administration updates its own file. Local governments may or may not submit records properly. And in the middle of that bureaucratic mess sits a state Medicaid office, now under federal orders to "fix it" or else.

So what happens? Anyone who vaguely resembles a match in these incomplete death records gets flagged. One wrong digit in a Social Security number, one typo in a birthdate, and suddenly someone very much alive finds themselves removed from coverage. Alive but unresponsive? Must be dead. Denied, cut off, good luck proving otherwise.

And don't expect a friendly phone call. This is Medicaid, not concierge service. You get a form letter—if the system sends one at all—and then you're stuck trying to reapply from scratch, in a system that's already overburdened and underfunded. You can try to call, but you'll be on hold for hours. Or days. And that's if the phone system hasn't collapsed under a surge of similar "errors."

Then we move to the "deceased providers" clause. That's right—this bill isn't just obsessed with dead patients. It wants the ghosts out of the provider network too. Some hospitals and clinics—especially in rural areas—get flagged for billing under credentials that haven't been updated. Doctors who've retired, moved, or passed away might still be listed on rosters, even if the services are being delivered by a new physician under the same practice.

So the bill tells states to clean that up too. Again, not unreasonable. But again, completely unfunded. States now have to upgrade systems that don't exist, run verification checks they can't afford, and field audits on billing data that may be years behind. The result? More paperwork. More vendor contracts. More time wasted on fixing billing anomalies that are symptoms of a broken infrastructure, not malicious fraud.

And let's not kid ourselves about the motive. This isn't about reclaiming wasted dollars. It's about appearances. Lawmakers want to be able to stand in front of cameras and say they've "cleaned up Medicaid," when all they've really done is put a filter on a cracked lens.

But the real damage comes from the incentives baked into the bill. If a state doesn't act fast enough to eliminate "ineligible" recipients or overpayments, they lose money. Federal matching funds get reduced. Administrative reimbursements dry up. That's not encouragement—that's extortion. It's the bureaucratic equivalent of saying, "Clean your house, or we burn it down."

So what do states do? They start preemptively denying or terminating coverage for any case that smells the least bit off. If a beneficiary doesn't respond to a mailer in time? Gone. If their income spikes briefly due to seasonal work? Gone. If they miss a recertification deadline because the form was mailed to the wrong address? You guessed it—gone.

And who gets hit hardest? The same groups that always do. The elderly with cognitive decline who can't navigate the system. Immigrants with language barriers and limited digital access. People experiencing housing insecurity who move too often to catch every piece of mail. They fall through the cracks not because they did anything wrong, but because the system was engineered to have cracks.

This is not cleanup. This is a purge wrapped in a press release. It's the weaponization of bureaucracy, using "efficiency" as a blunt instrument to do what no politician wants to say out loud: shrink the rolls, reduce spending, and let attrition do the dirty work.

And there's one more twist—the bill gives the federal government new oversight power. If they think your state isn't doing a good enough job scrubbing the rolls, they can intervene. They can cut funding. They can mandate corrective action plans. In other words, the same federal government that's underfunding your systems can then punish you for those systems failing. It's Kafka meets HHS.

But don't worry, it's all in the name of "program integrity." The phrase gets repeated like a spell throughout the bill, as if saying it often enough will make it true. But here's the reality: the program wasn't collapsing under the weight of deceased enrollees. The fraud rate wasn't exploding. What was growing was enrollment—because people need healthcare. That's the part lawmakers didn't like.

So rather than admit they wanted to reduce access, they invented a cleanliness crisis. And now state Medicaid directors are stuck trying to scrub a system with a toothbrush while being told to cut costs, avoid errors, and keep their hands tied.

This chapter isn't just about spreadsheets and systems. It's about values. It's about whether we believe access to care is worth defending even when the process gets messy. Because life is messy. People are messy. Bureaucracy is always messy. But stripping coverage in the name of cleanup isn't fixing the mess—it's burning the file cabinet and declaring the room organized.

And while lawmakers pat themselves on the back for eliminating "waste," millions of Americans will quietly lose coverage. Not because they didn't qualify. Not because they didn't need it. But because they couldn't keep up with a system designed to fail them.

That's the Medicaid "cleanup" in this bill. It doesn't polish. It doesn't improve. It erases—efficiently, mechanically, and without a trace of shame.

Chapter 9: Medicaid Payment Penalties

This chapter is where the bill stops pretending to care about "better outcomes" and shows its real face: budget enforcement at gunpoint. Forget about improving care or ensuring access. This section exists for one reason only—to turn state Medicaid agencies into financial scapegoats.

It starts with a simple premise that's made to sound responsible: if a state is making "excess payments," the federal government will reduce the amount it sends them. Sounds reasonable, right? Don't overpay, and you'll be fine. Except what counts as "excess" is a moving target—and the feds are holding the ruler.

We're not talking about fraud here. That's a separate issue, with its own enforcement channels. This is about administrative inconsistencies, data mismatches, and minor coding errors— anything that makes it look like too much money went to a provider or a patient. Doesn't matter if the care was real. Doesn't matter if the patient needed it. If it gets flagged as excessive, the federal match gets cut.

What does that mean in practice? If a state reimburses for a service that the federal system says wasn't fully documented— or was billed slightly outside the standardized rate structure— bam, penalty. If their systems don't line up perfectly with federal databases? Penalty. If they follow an older policy that hasn't been updated in the CMS guidance yet? You guessed it—penalty.

And these aren't small nudges. We're talking about multi-million dollar hits to state budgets, which are already being asked to do more with less. So what happens next? States start doing what any rational actor does under threat of punishment—they get defensive. They start underpaying providers. They start slow-walking reimbursements. They second-guess approvals. They delay care.

Because in this system, errors don't cost providers or vendors or contractors. They cost the state. So the state turns around and insulates itself the only way it can: by making access harder, benefits leaner, and services slower. It's a downward spiral with patients stuck in the middle.

And let's not forget the systemic reality: Medicaid's payment systems are a mess. Legacy software, manual overrides, conflicting codes between state and federal systems—all baked in from decades of underinvestment. So when the feds say "get your payments right," what they really mean is "go fix a machine we've all broken and do it without any new funding."

To make this even more absurd, the bill tightens the leash on how often states must redetermine eligibility, just as they're being punished for making overpayments. So the incentive becomes clear: keep people off the rolls, and your payment risk goes down. That's not policy. That's gaming the system under threat of financial strangulation.

Now, states aren't dumb. They see where this is going. They know that any payment even vaguely out of compliance could get flagged. So what do they do? They start demanding more documentation. More third-party verification. More signatures. More proof that the patient is real, the service was provided, the doctor is licensed, the invoice is within range, and the stars were aligned just right.

It's not about fraud prevention. It's about risk management. States are managing to the audit, not to the patient. The care itself becomes secondary. The priority is making sure nobody in Washington can say, "Hey, you overpaid by 0.8% last quarter." Because that 0.8% could cost the state millions.

So providers adapt too. They either raise their prices to offset delayed payments, or they leave Medicaid altogether. In rural areas or underserved urban clinics, this can be a death sentence. If you're a patient on Medicaid and your provider stops accepting it, your choices are: travel, wait, or go without. That's not access. That's abandonment dressed in federal compliance.

And none of this improves efficiency. It just shifts the burden. The bill doesn't give states better tools, clearer definitions, or modernized systems. It gives them penalties. That's it. It punishes them for navigating a system that was already too complicated to run without error.

Let's be honest about who this helps. It's not patients. It's not providers. It's certainly not the state agencies whose staff are burning out under piles of compliance paperwork. The only beneficiaries are the lawmakers who can now brag about "cracking down on Medicaid waste" while ignoring the chaos they've created.

This isn't oversight. It's extortion with a calculator.

And remember, all of this is happening in a program that already operates on the thinnest possible margins. Medicaid reimbursements are notoriously low. Administrative budgets are already stretched. Staff turnover is high. And now states are told to clean house or forfeit cash, using tools that haven't been updated since the Bush administration.

Worse still, the bill offers no clear remediation path. If you get penalized, there's no transparent appeal process. No arbitration. Just less money next quarter. Figure it out. Try harder. Work smarter. All the clichés without the funding, training, or structural changes to make them possible.

This isn't about fixing anything. It's about offloading responsibility. The feds want lower Medicaid costs on the books without taking the political heat for cutting people off directly. So they pass that burden to the states, bury it in compliance metrics, and call it reform.

And just in case you think this is a one-time squeeze, the bill makes it repeatable. Quarterly evaluations. Ongoing penalties. No sunset clause. Just an endless feedback loop of audit, penalize, cut, repeat.

Here's the real translation: if you're a state and your systems aren't perfect—and none are—you now live under constant financial threat. And your safest path forward isn't to improve care. It's to reduce exposure. Which means fewer approvals. Lower benefits. Less risk. And a Medicaid program that looks more like a tax form than a lifeline.

That's what this chapter builds: a risk-averse, audit-driven Medicaid machine that fears overpayment more than it values coverage. Where getting it wrong costs money, and getting it right offers no reward. Where patients are liabilities, not constituents. And where success is measured not in outcomes—but in how few people slip past the compliance net.

That's not accountability. It's sabotage dressed up as stewardship. And it's only just begun.

Chapter 10: Medicaid Asset Test Tightened

This chapter delivers the final gut punch to one of the last remaining illusions in American social policy—that you can be poor enough to need help and still hang on to a shred of financial security. The new Medicaid asset rules don't just tighten eligibility—they grind it into a pulp and dare you to fight back.

Let's start with the house. Under current Medicaid law, if your home is worth more than a certain threshold, you may be disqualified from receiving long-term care benefits. The idea is that Medicaid shouldn't foot the bill for someone who can theoretically sell off a high-value home to pay for their nursing care. Reasonable on its surface—until you realize the thresholds have been low, uneven, and entirely disconnected from actual housing markets.

Now this bill changes the threshold again. It raises the ceiling in theory, offering states more "flexibility." But buried in that word is the catch: states are now *allowed* to set their own lower limits, even below the new federal maximum. Translation: this isn't about helping more people qualify—it's about giving states the green light to disqualify more of them under the banner of "fiscal responsibility."

And let's be clear—this won't touch the wealthy. They don't use Medicaid for long-term care. They've got private insurance, trust funds, and shell corporations for that. This hits the middle—the retiree with a modest, paid-off home in a market that appreciated faster than they did. The working-class homeowner who finally crawled into a piece of property after a lifetime of renting. The widow in the house she and her husband bought in 1972.

In other words, this is about punishing people for owning the only asset that kept them afloat. If that house is over the state's new limit? Sell it. Refinance it. Go into debt. Drain your equity. Or go without care. Those are your options now. Independence or eligibility—but not both.

The moral rot here is staggering. The federal government is telling people: you can be poor in every other way, but if you dared to hold onto a house, we're counting that against you. It's a penalty for stability. A tax on having endured.

And it doesn't end there. This provision opens the door for even more aggressive estate recovery practices. If you receive long-term care services through Medicaid and you die with a home still in your name, the state can seize it to recoup costs. That's not new. But under the new rules, more people will fall under these terms—thanks to stricter eligibility, more forced disclosures, and a tighter definition of exempt property.

So much for the "family home." It's a liability now. An asset to be liquidated before you're allowed to be helped. Because heaven forbid Medicaid cover your care while your children inherit a roof over their heads.

Let's not forget the bureaucratic gauntlet this creates. Home value isn't a static number. It fluctuates with the market. So who's assessing that value? Which assessor? Which database? What happens when Zillow says your house is worth $280,000 but the county tax rolls say $210,000? Which one does the state use? Whichever one disqualifies you, probably.

And what if you live in a rural area where your house wouldn't sell for half its assessed value? Too bad. Paper value is what counts. Not whether you can actually extract that value without becoming homeless.

These changes also undermine intergenerational wealth transfer. Not for the elite, who shelter their wealth in trusts and LLCs. But for working families, the home *is* the inheritance. It's the only thing passed down, often because there's nothing else. This bill tells them: you get nothing. Not because you didn't work. Not because you didn't sacrifice. But because you asked for care and dared to still own something.

And here's where it gets crueler: this provision also incentivizes misinformation. Desperate families will start hiding ownership. Putting homes in the names of relatives. Creating shady "life estate" deals. Not because they want to cheat the system, but because the system is designed to strip them bare before it offers help. So now you'll get a wave of disqualifications based on incomplete disclosures—followed by appeals, audits, and more denial.

It's death by paperwork. A calculated strategy to make the process too complicated, too invasive, and too risky for people to even try. Better to go without than to lose your house. And for many, that's exactly the choice they'll face.

This chapter is dressed in fiscal prudence, but it's nothing more than economic eugenics by spreadsheet. It says to working people, "You can age in place, or you can age with care—but not both." Pick one. And when you don't? Don't worry. We've got a place for you on the waitlist.

There's a reason this provision was buried deep in the bill. It doesn't poll well. People don't like being told that their biggest lifetime asset is a barrier to healthcare. So it had to be wrapped in language like "asset threshold adjustments" and "state flexibility." But don't be fooled. This is theft, sanctioned by legislation.

The American promise—such as it ever was—wasn't built on luxury. It was built on stability. A job, a home, a retirement plan that didn't involve panic. This bill guts that promise. It says you can work your whole life, play by the rules, and still get screwed at the finish line.

Because now, the system doesn't just ask what you need. It asks what you own. And if the answer is "too much," the door slams shut.

This isn't reform. It's liquidation. And it's coming for the people who thought they'd earned a margin of safety. The homeowners. The caretakers. The barely-making-it retirees. They thought the house meant security.

Turns out, it just made them a target.

Chapter 11: Immigrant and Emergency Medicaid Limits

Let's stop pretending this is about tightening a budget. This is about drawing a circle around who's deserving of healthcare—and who isn't. It's not fiscal prudence. It's ideological boundary-setting.

First up: lawful status. Under this bill, Medicaid becomes a fortress exclusively for citizens, green-card holders, a few Cubans and Haitians, and Compact of Free Association residents. Everyone else—temporary workers, DACA recipients, asylum seekers—get shut out. The message is clear: your presence, your taxes, your health needs—none of it matters unless your paperwork fits a narrow definition.

It's not incidental that mixed-status families get hit hardest. Even if those ineligible individuals receive no benefits, *their* income still counts against the household. You file taxes, pay your premiums, but the government pretends you make more than you do—just to justify denying coverage to your U.S.-born child. That's not policy. That's punitive accounting.

Worse: emergency Medicaid remains. A bare-bones, triage-only patch. You can get emergency treatment—but only immediate life-or-limb interventions. Massively expensive surgical crisis? Yes. A clogged heart artery? Yes. Ongoing diabetic care? No. Preventative visits? Forget it. Chronic conditions? Prepare for hospital stays or death.

It's a brutal truth: emergency Medicaid is about the federal government protecting itself from liability, not offering real care. It shifts medical costs to local safety nets, emergency rooms—places that will bill upwards of twenty times what a primary care visit costs. Taxpayers, meanwhile, foot the bill anyway, just later.

Let's talk enforcement. States aren't taking applications at this point. They're deploying caseworkers trained to flag immigration status, verify documentation, cross-check visa expiration dates. If your green card expired—even accidentally—your whole household gets reorganized. The government is chasing date stamps instead of disease outcomes, and people who make clerical errors get hurt first.

And no, this is not hypothetical. We've seen this before: Medicaid chill. Immigrant families avoiding care out of fear— even when their citizen kids qualify. They know the drill: a visit to the doctor, and the whole family gets entangled in status reviews. This doesn't stop that. It amplifies it.

But the bill doesn't stop there. It also stops asylum seekers from getting work authorization while waiting for their cases. The logic, according to campaign lines, is "no work without status." The result? People who are already off the rolls become destitute. Unable to work, ineligible for primary care, terrified of being seen. It's a punishment inventory: first your access, then your agency, then your dignity.

Then there's the transit ban. You crossed a third country without applying for asylum there? Tough luck. You're ineligible. The border policy gets nationalized. No matter if the third country was unsafe or your entry was involuntary. No case-by-case exceptions. It's blanket exclusion.

Asylum is being restructured from a humanitarian reset to a logistical rejection. Credits, caps, bans—all wrapped in the language of "streamlining" and "enforcement." But any lawyer worth their salt will tell you: due process needs time. Fast-tracked deportation is the exact opposite. It's theatre.

Worse still: the bill lets state attorneys general sue the federal government for any enforcement they deem lax. That means red, blue, and purple states can weaponize federalism to drive their own exclusion agendas—no legislative bridge required. Have a state AG who wants to punish DACA kids? Write a letter, file a lawsuit, watch new statewide restrictions appear.

And because legal entry and asylum are tighter, migration pressure builds at the border. What happens then? The bill authorizes National Guard deployments in border states—without federal sign-off. That's not policy. That's occupation by mandate. It escalates tension, militarizes communities, and normalizes what should be an extreme measure: border troops inside the U.S.

This is border policy by posture. It's performative. Aggressive. Designed to look hard while imposing vague "border security" terms in perpetuity. It's the wedge mentality rendered into legislation—no citizenship pathway, no refuge. Just levels of exclusion.

But here's the kicker: none of this is about managing migration. Remittances still flow. Seasonal labor still happens. Families still move. The law doesn't calibrate migration. It restructures the safety net. It deters use. It co-opts moral panic. It sets the terms of belonging.

This chapter does not improve public health. It doesn't help integration. All it does is take what little care migrant communities had and clip it to the bone—under the perverse logic that if we make it harder to get help, they'll just leave. But they don't leave. They stay. They work. And they get sicker. They show up in emergency rooms with uncontrolled conditions, unpaid bills, and broken trust in a system designed to build that very distrust.

At the end of the day, every cut, every complex rule, every siloed exception—it's not about saving money. It's about building a moral firewall, visible or invisible, around citizenship and care. This is not governance. It's gatekeeping—layered, bureaucratic, and cruel.

That's not reform. That's exclusion under law. And in this bill, it's freed from any pretense of humanitarian concern. Welcome to Medicaid, redefined by fear.

Chapter 12: Long-Term Care Staffing Freeze

Let's be blunt: this chapter isn't about protecting seniors—it's about shielding nursing home owners and operators from accountability. The federal staffing mandates, forged in the wake of COVID's carnage, promised basic standards: enough nurses, enough aides, enough eyes on residents to catch neglect before it became fatal. Now those mandates are paused, frozen in legal amber. Medicaid and Medicare long-term care facilities can operate with fewer staff, fewer oversight visits, and fewer consequences.

When regulators talk about "usability" or "flexibility," they're not honoring the elderly—they're cutting costs. Staffing ratios, care hour minimums, mandatory shift coverage—all sidelined. Facilities are being told: use your judgment. Which, in practice, means cutting corners to keep your bottom line attractive to investors.

Here's how the real world reacts: nursing homes fire or don't replace staff under rare vacancies. Call lights go unanswered longer. Family visits catch residents dehydrated, confused, or incontinent because there simply weren't enough people to help them. Medication errors rise. Bedsores emerge. These aren't hypothetical tragedies—they're everyday outcomes travelling unnoticed in a system that costs less when nobody counts standards.

Let's not mince words—this isn't about bureaucratic hassle. This is about valuing profit over people. With mandates frozen, owners can claim they're "adapting to local needs" or "navigating workforce shortages." But here's the truth: locals will adapt to neglect. Workers who are exhausted will keep working. Families who want comfort for loved ones will settle. No one writes in a care standard when the board cares about quarterly returns.

The pretext is that staffing mandates are too rigid, too standardized, one-size-fits-all. The counterpoint: thousands died because there wasn't enough staff to manage infection control or conduct daily check-ins. That wasn't politics—it was policy failure. Freezing these rules tells every facility that the death of the elderly is collateral damage, not a failure.

Policies don't die in crisis—they transform. And what this chapter does is shift responsibility upward—away from owners and operators—while pushing blame onto downstream entities: states, staffing agencies, families. It says: we gave you rules, you can't enforce them, but we won't penalize you if you opt-out. If someone dies, that's saddening—but legal.

That's how quietly you dismantle standards without abandoning them entirely. No announcement. No debate. Just a clause saying "pause enforcement." And suddenly a system that required daily observation can survive on daily visits instead of live-ins. A facility can schedule nursing coverage just for weekdays rather than evenings or weekends. You can convert RN positions into LPN or aide roles without exceeding federal guidelines. You can classify staff as "on-call" instead of physically present.

But there's no substitute for human presence. After sunset, when doors are locked and hallways empty, people bill, slip, or wander. Without staff, there's nobody to notice. And even when something is noticed, a freeze means inspectors can't tag it as a violation. They can offer recommendations—but no penalties. Which means no urgency. Which means silence wins.

Let's talk incentives. Facilities are audited, yes—but definitions of compliance have changed. Now, being "staffed" means "didn't fail an emergency drill." It has nothing to do with actual care. That's by design. If ease of regulation equals regulatory safety, assume they wrote it that way for maximal benefit. And nobody is advocating for re-checks or surprise audits. Once the freeze is in place, there's no safety valve.

The bill buries this change under layers of budget language: freeze staffing mandates, realign care standards, provide flexibility under Title X. But it's not flexibility. It's abdication. It's emptying the safety cushion while pretending responsibility hasn't changed.

Now consider public funding. Medicaid and Medicare pay these facilities—some of the richest reimbursement rates in the system—for long-term care. You'd think that'd come with obligations. But this bill reverses portions of that logic: receive public money, but face no public standards. Providing less service is acceptable. No sanction. No refund. No accountability.

This encourages consolidation. Small local homes can't justify staffing without standards—they go bust or get bought. Large chains operate with the same staffing they had pre-COVID, optimized for profitability, not minimum care. That's how we end up with communities with one "affordable" long-term-care option—an option that's quietly subsisting on facilities built for years ago when families paid, and oversight meant something.

Don't believe for a second that non-profit chains fare better. Non-profits operate by the same rules. No mandate, no penalty, no compliance. They may still try to maintain standards—they may even say they do—but when push comes to shove, board decisions weigh quality against survival. And with budgets squeezed, survival wins. At best, "quiet compliance" is seen as "cost-effective caregiving."

Finally, let's consider the timing. This chapter isn't front-loaded. It phases in when public attention is elsewhere—

during fiscal quarters when reporters won't dig. It's hidden until months after passage. And by then facilities are "adapted." Boards have adjusted. Staffing pools have shrunk under demand. Gone are the RNs. Gaps are filled with aides. Facilities look around and say, "We expected this."

They expected wrong. In robust systems, suction and resource compression balance out—they don't destroy safety nets. Here, the balance sheet is final. Care capacity shrinks. Risk to residents rises. Families are told to trust facilities, even when oversight is removed.

This isn't reform. It's dilution. It's a resignation of responsibility. And it shows the moral architecture of the bill: cut the middle, take the edges—the measurement, the minimum, the safeguard—leave people struggling to defend themselves in what's supposed to be a care environment. Welcome to the freeze that freezes lives.

Chapter 13: Reduced Provider Incentives

Here's where the bill's economic architecture gets sly: by gutting the financial tools states rely on to make Medicaid work, it proves once again that the problem wasn't waste or fraud—it was demand. States aren't wrestling with inefficiency—they're wrestling with real need. And this chapter cuts their budget rope.

Enter provider taxes and directed payments—gimmicks? No. These were pragmatic solutions crafted when automatic federal match rates weren't enough to keep hospitals, clinics, and nursing homes afloat. States taxed providers, lost minimal revenue, then matched it with federal funds. The net result: hospitals in underserved areas stayed open, safety-net clinics stayed staffed, and home care agencies kept their lights on. Doctors tolerated it because they still got paid and patients still got treated.

This bill slashes those workarounds. It limits what states can do with provider taxes. It narrows eligibility for directed payments—those extra reimbursements states could give to critical-access facilities, rural providers, or behavioral health systems. The message? If the federal government won't fully fund your needs, don't look for alternatives. We're closing the loopholes.

Let's be blunt: this isn't fiscal discipline. It's disinvestment. States don't have infinite budgets. Take away the provider taxes and directed payments, and hospitals lose money. They stop serving Medicaid patients. Or worse, they close. That's not exaggeration—it's math.

To make matters worse, the bill raises the financial bar for what states can call a demonstration project. Remember when states experimented with care coordination, integrated mental-health services, or managed long-term care? Those pilots came with provider flexibility. They worked because they allowed local solutions. Now the bill retrofits those pilots with rules requiring cost-neutrality upfront. You want to test a better way to treat opioid addiction? Prove it won't cost more—today, tomorrow, or ever. That's not innovation. That's paralysis.

Of course, the bill tosses a bone to states with discretionary grants and a hope-it-helps clause. But these small sums can't replace tens or hundreds of millions channeled through provider taxes that drew matching federal dollars. It's like telling someone to balance their budget on ramen money after taking away their paycheck.

The endgame: healthcare deserts expand. Rural communities lose their clinics. Urban safety nets shrink. Behavioral and mental-health services evaporate. And the sick, the poor, and the isolated lose again—not because someone stole money, but because they needed it.

Consider the reflexology of this provision: states induced into compliance by budget shortfall, hospitals laying off staff or shutting units, patients finding fewer options or longer waits. Then, politicians point to the empty clinic and say: "See? Medicaid failed." But it's not Medicaid that failed. It's Congress. Congress that 'fixed' Medicaid by removing the very tools states needed to fund healthcare.

And remember: provider incentives benefited almost no one with punchy political ads. They weren't sexy. They didn't sell. So they got slashed quietly. Good luck running a state healthcare system on cuts and clichés.

This chapter doesn't reform Medicaid. It starves it. And when services dry up, it won't be because someone added more blood to the waterline—it'll be because someone said "this is how it has to be." And when communities collapse under the weight of attention starvation, nobody will ask why we left them on their knees.

That's the relentless logic of this bill: cut structural supports, blame local managers, and punish the vulnerable. And we call it "integrity."

Chapter 14: Budget-Neutral Pilot Projects Only

Let's call this clause what it truly is: a prohibition on innovation dressed up as fiscal prudence. Federal Medicaid's former "waiver" system allowed states a little breathing room—to pilot new care strategies, test community-based interventions, or integrate health and social services. Those projects cost money up front, sure. But they often paid dividends later with better outcomes and long-term savings. This bill rewrites the rule: if it isn't budget-neutral before it starts, don't bother.

Budget-neutral from day one. That's an absurd standard. Health innovation isn't a zero-sum game; it involves upfront investment and delayed return. Requiring self-funded innovation before benefits materialize ensures nothing new ever takes root. Behavioral health coordinators, integrated primary-care models, telehealth for rural patients—those may be sensible, evidence-based ideas. But under this mandate, they're dead in the water unless a treasury-certified accountant approves them upfront.

So what happens instead? States simply stop proposing pilots. They risk a letter from Treasury saying they miscalculated their future savings outlook. They can't chance losing federal matching funds midstream. State legislatures, which provide real oversight, are cut out entirely. No local input. No incremental testing. No flexibility.

Let's be honest: if politicians actually wanted to improve Medicaid, they'd make innovation easier. They'd manufacture incentives, seed grants, shared-savings initiatives. Instead, this bill erects a dam. It tells states: you want to try something new? Guarantee it costs nothing. Oh, and do it in the middle of a staffing freeze, payment penalty regime, eligibility crackdown, and asset test expansion.

This isn't policy. It's paralysis. Innovation isn't dead—it's legislatively murdered here. Welcome to a future where Medicaid programs can't evolve, adapt, or respond to local needs. Care is frozen in amber. And control remains centralized, rigid, and remarkably stupid.

Want outcomes? Want efficiency? Want smarter care? Not here. Not now. Not ever. Everything must fit the existing budget—or don't bother proposing it in the first place.

That's the result when the system values auditability over adaptability. You pass chapters on eligibility and cost, enforce them with deadlines and penalties, and then lock the exits. So congratulations—you've built a cage. Medicaid stays alive, but it won't grow. And America will pay for nothing but mediocrity pretending to be reform.

Chapter 15: Medicaid Work and Cost-Sharing Rules

This chapter strips away any pretense that Medicaid exists to support public health or accountability. Instead, it repackages poverty as a moral failure and dangles aid as if it were a reward for perfect paperwork and passive compliance. The architects of this legislation want you to think this is about improving outcomes or instilling fiscal discipline. It's not. It's about control, about shrinking enrollment and maintaining the image of reform while the system quietly punishes those who come too close.

Let's start with work requirements. On the surface, these sound sensible: able-bodied adults without dependents—under-65, without disability—must meet monthly work or volunteer-hour targets or lose access. It's sold as a nudge toward employment and self-reliance, but that framing ignores the real-world conditions. Most people on Medicaid who can work already do, often in part-time or variable-hour jobs. What they don't have is consistent hours, a reliable schedule, or access to approved training programs. Stories of needing to log 80 documented hours per month may sound doable on TV, but they don't hold up against the complexities of gig labor, caregiving, transportation gaps, health setbacks, or scheduling volatility. This rule doesn't lift people; it locks them out.

The exemptions read like a checklist of sympathy but function as bureaucratic landmines. Yes, pregnant women, caregivers, disabled individuals, elders, and tribal members are exempt—at least in theory. But the system forces the burden of proof back onto the applicant. Show us your documentation. Prove your status. And do it on time. Miss a doctor's note? A court order? A tribal ID? You're non-compliant. This isn't compassion; it's coercion. Seek compliance or face exclusion, and don't expect leniency.

Then there's the enforcement mechanism—state-level. The feds shift responsibility down and say, "Make it happen." States, terrified of losing federal funding if their compliance rate drops, respond by tightening eligibility standards, denying borderline cases, delaying renewals, and performing audits. It's a recipe for wider churn: people go on and off Medicaid not because their need changed, but because their paperwork didn't pass muster. And when they're off, they lose primary care access, fall behind on meds, end up in the ER—and the cycle costs more than the program saved by denying them.

This chase for administrative precision is baked into the law. If a state registers fatal drops in compliance or caveats in enforcement, federal matching funds dry up—quarterly, not yearly. That's effectively a cliff: either you enforce perfectly, or we pull the rug. So states don't strengthen healthcare—they strengthen rejection processes. That's not policy optimization; it's perverse incentive design.

Now, this carries into cost-sharing. Medicaid recipients live on the edge. This chapter introduces co-pays for doctor visits, small premiums, prescription fees, and deductibles. Under a public health lens, these should be counterproductive: you raise the price of care, people avoid it, health worsens, costs rise in crisis. But that's the point. Expressed in policy-speak, the goal is to instill "responsibility." But interpreted on the ground, it looks like this: you owe a dollar? You don't pay? You risk being dropped.

It's a behavioral economic whittling. Volume co-pays or premiums become subtle hurdles that turn into insurmountable walls, especially for those living paycheck to paycheck. One missed payment leads to suspension, and then reinstatement becomes another bureaucratic gauntlet.

Combine cost-sharing with work mandates, and you get operational chaos. People cycle in and out with changing incomes, job hours, and paperwork. The human toll is invisible in cost-benefit spreadsheets, where churn equals efficiency. But ask any caseworker, and they'll tell you the flip side: increasing churn costs more money, time, and moral authority than maintaining stable coverage. A denied claim, a missed renewal, even a brief gap in care can spiral into cumulative damage— unmanaged chronic conditions, higher hospital readmissions, declines in mental health.

That isn't just collateral damage; it's baked into the legislative architecture. The bill creates deliberate friction, because reducing enrollments data-wise looks like progress, while actual human suffering is dismissed as "off the books." This is not reform. It's denial by design.

Now, imagine you live in rural America, working part-time at a diner. Hours vary weekly. No paid sick days. Transportation demands you shift your route often. Your rent gets paid sporadically. You can't always make that co-pay. You miss a renewal letter. The state flags your non-compliance—and boom—you're cut. You wander into a hospitalization six months later because a diabetic condition went unchecked.

The cost is triple what managing your care would have been. Your state pays fines, your community pays charity bills, and the feds shrug!

It gets worse: by stamping these rules as permanent—and removing flexibility or waivers—the bill ensures that no matter who controls state government, compliance remains rigid. No carve outs during recessions, pandemics, or regional crises. When unemployment spikes, as it will, people won't get breathing room. They'll get purged.

So why go to these lengths? Because the political optics of "lower Medicaid rolls" are easier to sell than the politics of investing in social infrastructure. Reducing benefits enables spectacle and sound bites: "We enforced discipline." "We restored balance." "We didn't expand entitlements." All without mentioning that fewer people got healthcare, conditions worsened for many, and local safety-net services collapsed under the weight.

Understand this: if policymakers were serious about improving outcomes, they'd invest in job training, childcare, transit vouchers, health navigators, community behavioral support— all proven to support employment and health simultaneously. But this bill does none of that. Instead, it punishes failure without providing support and labels attrition as success.

The result is that Medicaid becomes a punitive compliance ledger. No longer a safety net, but a test of bureaucratic gymnastics. And for those who fail—intentionally or by accident—there's no mercy clause. Just termination. Not because they don't deserve help, but because the system prioritized appearance over service.

So let's call this what it is: Session fifteen of a long-running performance of austerity in motion. A policy that repackages social withdrawal as fiscal discipline, moral ascent, employer engagement, or budgetary salvation. It repurposes paperwork as a virtue signifier and churn as an achievement metric.

Every line of this chapter shrinks Medicaid through policy friction, not through meaningful reform. And that friction doesn't happen by accident; it was designed into the system to exclude quietly and follow up with applause later. This is policy with intention. Not intention to help, but intention to deny.

Chapter 16: Green Energy Rollbacks and Fossil Fuel Favoritism

This chapter doesn't ambush green energy with subtle punting—it nuke-launches clean energy policy while decking fossil fuel interests in the name of energy independence. Strip away the PR language about "balanced portfolios" and what you have is a scorched earth redux of 21st-century climate efforts, revealed as the artful destruction of forward momentum. They aren't just retracting incentives; they're actively empowering archaic industries at the expense of progress—and they want applause for it.

On paper, it starts like a game developer's Easter egg. Clean energy tax credits—EV purchases, residential solar installations, commercial green hydrogen, advanced manufacturing credits, charging stations—poof, gone. Every meaningful incentive born in recent climate-focused legislation gets repealed or sunsetted. That means homeowners contemplating solar rebates get zilch. Electric car buyers recalculating their cost just to get priced out. Developers waiting on wind and battery investments learn that their cost-of-capital just went up overnight—no glow, no credit, no forward path. It's a deliberate dismantling of markets that were just gaining traction.

Simultaneously, the bill drops a loaded coin in the fossil-fuel slot. Production tax credits, intangible drilling cost deductions, categorization shifts, redefinition: all steering capital and corporate strategy toward oil, gas, and other extractive energy sectors. For fossil companies, this is economic doping written into tax code. This is not a transition to cleaner energy; it's a rigged extension of backward subsidies. They even extend Section 45 credit equivalents to biogas and natural gas, framing gas infrastructure as a partial environmental solution. Never mind that leaks and lifecycle carbon are ignored, climate modeling dismissed, and long-term emissions unmanaged. It's talk dressed in the veneer of pragmatism.

Now, the retrospective here would be easier to swallow if this looked like balance. But it doesn't. Clean energy receives nickel-and-diming caps; fossil fuel gets full, streamlined expansion. EV credits are eliminated entirely. Oil and gas get deductions for exploration, drilling, transportation, and storage. This isn't a policy pivot—it's a full-scale reallocation of public money from the future to the past. Underneath every clause is a whisper: "You want democracy in energy? Then pay for it." And implicitly, "Or else."

The runaway is intentional. As clean energy industries contract, fossil industries expand. Investors shift. Workers pivot. Infrastructure shifts to pipelines, drilling platforms, refineries—while solar and wind factories run empty and factories await permits they'll never get. The innovation ecosystem falters under punishing tax structure, job creation slows, and fossil fuel engineers find shiny new incentives to retool old rigs. That's not market mechanics—that's political architecture repurposed for preservation, at the expense of climate, environment, and long-term strategy.

The damage compounds when we consider advanced manufacturing. Electric vehicle production, semiconductor plants, battery development—industries central to global competitiveness—now run out of working capital because the credits and cost offsets that attracted them are overwritten. Places that were counting on shovel-ready projects in upstate New York or Texas find themselves high-and-dry. Politicians will credit their "pro-worker" stance, but the layoff lists and delayed openings tell the truth: they prioritized fossil-fuel profits over diversified resilient future industries.

What this chapter does is institutionalize decline. It takes advantage of timing—for fossil interests to reap short-term gains, for green innovation to hemorrhage capital. Regulation isn't just paused; it's structurally shifted. The tilt isn't subtle. It's tectonic. They've engineered a crash of green energy while providing a ramp-up for gas and oil lobbyists. The narrative? Energy independence. The result? Short-term PR headlines, long-term competitive decline, and an unspoken social contract resting on high-carbon returns.

Even the language of "transition" is weaponized. Clean hydrogen gets mentioned, but only as a footnote. Geothermal, nuclear—technologies once under the broader climate umbrella—are reduced to limited eligibility under public-traded partnerships. That's a bureaucratic trap. Limited liquidity for investors unless structured inside an oil-and-gas-compatible PTP. Technological options dwindle because every economic lever is tilted to keep fossil fuel dominant.

Now consider the existential message: if green energy needs government to survive—and this law jettisons that government support—what does anyone in those industries do? They recalibrate expectations. Projects shelved. Rollbacks enacted. Employees redeployed. EV price points readjusted. That's ignoring incentives—not neutral policymaking, but active disinvestment. It says, "We'll pay for drilling, but not diversification." It says, "You can help the climate—but you'll get no help here." It says, "We value yesterday more than tomorrow."

And what of side effects? Expect storms of economic damage. Urban manufacturers hurt. Rural communities lose solar manufacturing plants. Corporate board rooms gush over cost forecasting and energy policy. Workforces shrink, retirements accelerate, talent drains out. Renewable engineers pivot to consulting. That's not just economic—it's moral. We're institutionalizing a handicap on progress.

Of course, the bill is legal, passed, signed. But policy isn't just about legality. It's about effects. Politicians get to claim they delivered on "American energy leadership," while the consumers pay more for electricity, loose climate targets, and foreign competition rises. Narratives about independence overshadow reality: the U.S. just traded away clean-tech advantage for fossil-fuel subsidies that won't create as many jobs, won't sustain long-term profitability as the world turns green.

Notice, too, that there's no compensation or transition plan. Clean energy workers laid off don't get retraining or relocation benefits. Communities lose tax base. States try IRS codes to adjust structure. They get nothing. Support is rare—philanthropy, municipal bonds, federal grants—and insufficient to make up for purposeful disinvestment.

Why now? Because fossil industries see momentary advantage. Because political narratives about independence beat out scientific timeframes. Because someone had to finance the exit from the clean energy economy—without nakedly saying so. And because you can't say "we're investing $20 billion in green transition," but you *can* say you're "reviving" fossil production, and claim victory.

But this charade won't last. Markets adjust. Global competition moves ahead. Thousands of clean energy jobs—and the emissions reductions that go with them—are sacrificed. Prices rise for homeowners at the pump. Consumer energy bills rise. Federal deficits remain unchanged. All for a moment of glory in the fossil lobby. That's not bold strategy. It's a one-off portfolio reshuffle to bail out yesterday's guard while tomorrow's remains parked.

The final verdict is predictable: The country will eventually refund clean programs under pressure. Congressional reversal will happen. But not before trust has been damaged, capital has retreated, and the industry has lost years of investment. So yes, in the short term, fossil companies win. Investors, lobbyists, certain state economies win. But the long-term cost—economic stagnation, environmental collapse, militarized energy dependencies—is off the books compared to this "victory."

Make no mistake: this chapter of the bill was written to undercut climate action with political ease and legislative opacity. It doesn't ask for forgiveness. It asks for oblivion. Clean energy isn't just unsupported—it's politely erased. America didn't pivot to green. Congress pivoted to fossil. And that pivot will cost us all.

That isn't governance. It's grievance—a preference for yesterday's economy over tomorrow's reality, and a breathtaking choice not to lead.

Chapter 17: Student Loans, Education, and Borrowing Limits

This chapter is not an educational reform—it's a structural cordon around access to degrees and future mobility. What it does isn't reform: it restricts opportunity, penalizes aspiration, and enshrines debt ceilings into law, all while patting itself on the back as responsible governance.

The central blow lands on graduate-level borrowing. The bill enforces a total cap of $50,000 on federal loans for master's, Ph.D., and professional degrees—not per year, but in aggregate. That number is either laughable or cruel, depending on your financial baggage. In most private and even many public graduate programs—law, medicine, business, engineering—that amount covers a single semester. And yet the bill treats it like a limiting safety valve, ignoring how it functions more like a barrier for anyone without at least six figures in disposable income or family wealth.

They justify it as a measure to curb excessive tuition inflation. If students can't borrow unlimited money, supposedly schools will stop raising prices. That logic is both naïve and misinformed. Tuition inflation isn't driven by federal borrowing alone—it's driven by the market model of universities, administrative bloat, athletic arms races, and campus amenity competitions. Cap borrowing, and what happens? Universities still raise prices. Students scramble to private loans—with higher interest rates, less flexibility, and worse protection. The bill doesn't fix structural inflation; it forces weaker borrowers into credit traps and wealthier borrowers or institutions with deep-line scholarships to carry on.

Now layer on the limits to forgiveness programs. The bill constricts public service loan forgiveness, ramps up reporting requirements, and lengthens timelines for forgiveness eligibility. Fewer job types qualify. More hoops are added. What remains of the forgiveness landscape becomes harder to navigate and slower to deliver results. Again, the rhetorical defense is fiscal responsibility—but the effect is chilling: fewer people will plan public service careers, fewer will go into education, mental health, government, or nonprofits. We shrink the pool of potential teachers, counselors, and community health providers while pretending we're saving dollars. We're not. We're starving public goods.

Meanwhile, the bill deepens institutional accountability: colleges must now report graduate earnings tied to tuition costs. The theory is transparency will straighten out the mismatches—wife of school. But in reality, earnings vary by region, by job market, by career path. A social work graduate in rural America won't earn the same as one in New York City. But if her earnings don't meet the federal wage indicator, her school can be penalized or lose aid eligibility. That transfers risk to students — who may be priced out — and to public-serving institutions that can't promise coastal salary scales. The institutions coaching students into public service find themselves financially insecure, close programs, or start shifting classes toward vocational pipelines—beat capitulating to earnings metrics. The bill boasts "value for money," but forgets that value isn't always measurable in four-figure earnings—it's about public service, social capital, and community resilience. That doesn't fit in a spreadsheet.

The chapter also throttles schools with high dropout rates or large federal loan recipients who don't repay quickly. That mainly hits for-profit institutions and regional community colleges where return-on-investment is modest. But guess who else gets caught? State universities with expanding continuing-education programs for working adults, refugee resettlement programs, or vocational upskilling. Not every student has to chase the top 10 percent salary. The system is now biased against it.

The bill does throw crumbs to modern education models: expanded Pell eligibility for short-term credentials—coding boot camps, nursing certifications, technical trade programs. That's the only recognition that education models outside the four-year degree lifecycle exist. Yet the funding for that is tiny. The chapter threads the needle for vocationalism, but only for now. Any successful model could bleed out once scrutiny begins or budget dispensations lapse.

On the student services side, the bill tightens oversight of loan servicers. That means stricter performance metrics, standardized error reporting, and timelines for dispatching borrower statements. It's a response to real dysfunction—delayed processing, misapplied payments, misinformation. But unless new consequences accompany the oversight, it's a tech-band-aid on systemic failure. Borrowers still suffer from call-line delays, unresolved billing, and bureaucratic drift. Improvement hinges on operational investment—not oversight.

Then there's a subtlety: extension of ex-tax employer contributions to student loans and updated 529-qualified expense coverage. These provide modest help to individuals with workplace support and families with flexible 529 usage. But they augment privilege more than access. Employers who offer benefits already cater to middle and upper-middle-class professionals. And students working within those organizations, again, aren't the ones most squeezed. Families with no access to job-based aid or wealthy benefactors get zero advantage here.

Let's be blunt: this chapter reshapes education funding so that it favors self-sufficient, employed individuals with stable incomes already—while pushing younger, lower-income, or marginalized aspirants toward private finance with no protections. It shrinks public payments, tightens borrowing mechanics, restricts forgiveness, crawls over institutional accountability, and offers rhetorical support only to models that require fewer dollars because they serve fewer students.

If this were about ensuring value, it would uncap public loans subject to quality metrics, incentivize deep investment in low-income-first programs, and tie institutional funding to equitable access and graduation outcomes across demographic lines. It doesn't. It builds walls around access with phrases like "budget restraint" and "skin-in-the-game." It penalizes aspiration if it's not codified in high-paying, low-risk pathways.

In effect, the chapter locks the front door but does nothing to open windows. It structures educational ambition into debt boxes, devalues public service, and ensures that the ladder of opportunity gets shorter at precisely the rung where millions struggle to climb. Any benefits—extended 529 flexibility, employer aid, or Pell for training—are token. The architecture of restriction speaks much louder than the footnotes of aid.

This isn't an education strategy. It's a barrier strategy. A policy trap set with borrower illusions and institution-level threats. And like every installment in this bill, it masks attrition as reform and cost cuts as prudence. In truth, it's a tollgate erected on the Zillow path to a career, not a roadmap. And you pay the price before the opportunity even arrives.

Chapter 18: Immigration, Border, and Asylum Enforcement Changes

This chapter pivots the narrative about immigration from policy nuance to procedural maximalism, trading any nuance for sheer volume of enforcement. It doesn't augment the system with clarity or resources—it overwhelms it with rules, penalties, and begging-for-federal-asylum voodoo shows. Everything is written with the explicit assumption that the answer to movement across the border is never access—it's resistance.

At the center of this effort is border fencing. Actual wall construction restarts under federal mandate. That's right: existing appropriations are declared unstoppable, regardless of local impact, environmental costs, or international treaty concerns. They curtail even executive rollback authority—meaning any future administration that wants to pause or dismantle construction would have to go through Congress or the courts. This isn't about infrastructure or national security. It's about entrenching a political bluff that Illinois—or anyone else—can't undo. The wall is now baked into legislative rigor, as untouchable as any Senate compromise, and as automatic as appropriations.

Then there's Border Patrol funding. More agents, more detention centers, more surveillance. That means buses full of people, machines full of cameras, and facilities full of beds designed to cage human beings. The litigation, the infrastructure, the money—all of it serves one purpose: to expand the machinery of exclusion far beyond ports of entry. This is not pragmatic strategy; it's show-of-force policy.

The redefinition of asylum criteria is even more dangerous. "Transit bans"—that is, if an asylum seeker passed through another country without applying for asylum there, their claim is invalidated. The assumption is blunt: if you didn't file the paperwork before you came to the U.S., your claim is bad. This ignores the realities: political asylum in Mexico may be unsafe or unattainable for certain nationalities. Yet the bill mandates zero discretion. Hard stops. No exceptions. Not even humanitarian exemptions. Asylum becomes a process you applied to in a third country or you didn't deserve it. That's absurdity disguised as legal clarity.

At the same time, the legislation fast-tracks asylum processing. Not for benefit—more for removal. The clocks get shorter, timelines compressed, appeals minimised. Pre-existing case law on credible fear interviews is thrown out. Migrants will have less time to meet with lawyers, assemble documentation, or present their stories. Cases that once took months now take weeks. And if a case is incomplete? You're out. Next flight.

This chapter also hikes fees across the board—to apply for visas, to adjust status, to get work authorization, and to reinstate residency. That money has to come from somewhere, and it comes from applicants: students, religious workers, families, long-term legal immigrants. The pay-to-play fee structure becomes a form of wealth test. You want to stay in the country? You better write the check. And if you can't? You'll stay, but undocumented. Or you'll leave.

What compounds all of this is the catch-and-release ban. It prohibits Border Patrol from releasing undocumented immigrants with a court date when migrants arrive. Instead of temporary release, the default becomes detention or expedited removal. That's prison with paperwork—regardless of intent, who asked for asylum first, or whether the individual poses any threat. Again, arbitrary on purpose.

The bill goes further by pausing work authorization for certain asylum seekers. No window. No six-month grace. Just sit and wait until someone decides whether you deserve to work at all. The result is clear: economic marginalization in service of deterrence. We're talking about families forced into the informal labor economy or rendered dependent on food banks while they wait—and that's not a design flaw. It's a policy desire.

State attorneys general can now sue the federal government if they believe it isn't enforcing the immigration law as spelled in this bill. What does that mean in practice? California, Texas, and every state in between can aggressively litigate to block policies—or to enforce harsher ones. This creates unpredictable legal feedback loops: national policy becomes a patchwork of state-driven court orders. No uniformity, no predictability, only chaos.

And there's a provision that lets governors deploy the National Guard to enforce the border without federal approval. That means border militarization at the state level—chain of command bypassed, civilian oversight muddied, and national policy undercut by local politics. State-run militarization as default policy. No coordination, no federal control, no accountability.

This chapter isn't reform. It's escalation. The asylum system gets more traps than someone assembling flatpack furniture with no instructions. Each procedural shift—tighter definitions, shorter timelines, transit bans, elevated fees—is another barrier programmed in. The burden of compliance is surgical. It lies with individuals, not with the bureaucracy or policy architects.

State-level enforcement tools treat border security as a zero-sum spectacle. Walls, militarized agents, detained people, formal and informal patrols—it's policy as pageantry. Each element gains its own political thunder. Politicians get to claim

"I defended the border"—while the bureaucracy tries to record every step and litigate every move.

The outcome? Fewer legitimate asylum claims, more people stuck in limbo, more lawyers chasing paperwork deadlines, more families trapped in processing centers or reliant on illicit work. We shouldn't treat asylum seekers as a spreadsheet line item. But this chapter does, metaphorically and literally—dropping daily case caps into law, codifying timelines that expire rights, ripping due-process under the language of outsourcing.

Candidates for asylum now face layered deterrence—some legal, some logistical, some financial. The carrier of these walls, both brick and bureaucratic, is the system. And the system will be fast. It will cut jobs, delay wages, leave bills unpaid, split families. It's gaslighting implemented in code and dollars.

This isn't policy. It's a policy-blow. A weld of federal and state-level muscle intended to convince outsiders their hope won't stand. It functions less like law and more like signal: see and fear.

We're not evaluating border crossings. We're reinforcing territory—and signaling fear spells as legislative code.

Chapter 19: Legal Enforcement and Implementation Mechanics

If Chapter 18 was about revving up the machinery of exclusion, this one is the mechanics room where the gears get greased—for eternity. It's not sexy. It's not human. It's the paragraph-length paragraphs about deposits, deadlines, and dense enforcement tools. But this is where the law stops pretending it could be adjusted or repealed in the future and instead becomes a locked-down regime passing from generation to generation— without debate, without oversight, without mercy.

The first anchor is timing. The bill hasn't just rewritten policy—it's set future enforcement into legal stone. Tax changes, benefit adjustments, work requirements, asset tests: they all default to January 1, 2026. More cruelly, some of the heaviest Medicaid cuts don't take effect until 2027 or 2028. That looks like patience and planning—but it's actually a political time bomb. It signals that Congress won't have to answer for consequences until midterm election season, and by then, the authors are long gone. Policymakers wanted cushion, not compromise. And this gives them criminal elbow room when constituents start shouting.

Next, the time bombs are literal: sunset clauses. Senior deductions, Trump accounts, temporary student loan exemptions—they expire in five years unless reconfirmed. That's not transparency. It's headed for oblivion, masked as thrift. And it signals that every single "benefit" in this bill is provisional—meant to be fought for again, not trusted as enduring. The message to future legislators: here's your budget baseline, but don't count on a damn thing unless it has a sunset.

But here's where it gets cruel: agencies aren't allowed to delay or re-interpret any of this. The IRS, HHS, the Department of Education—all have to implement exactly what's written. No administrative flexibility in emergencies, crises, or statutory luridness. That clause looks reasonable until disaster strikes: if inflation spikes, if a pandemic returns, if border pressure swells—none of that can legally soften the blow. Agencies can't waiver. They can't pause. They can't interpret. They must do it verbatim. That's law as weapon, not guidance.

And if they don't? Enter the legal standing clause. States, individuals, even corporations can sue over non-enforcement. Want the wall completed? Sue. Need the asset test implemented? Sue. Want an exemption enforced? Sue. The long-term effect is litigious stalemate: everything is law, nothing is policy. Lawsuits await the earliest administrative misstep. Policy becomes litigated before implemented, and dysfunction is baked in. This isn't governance—it's governance-as-war.

Now, the sneaky outbreak is the requirement for bonds in legal challenges. You think you can bring a lawsuit against the government? Fine, post a bond. And not a symbolic one—enforcement actions, bond by bond, could require thousands or millions. And if you can't pay, the court won't even consider your case. That doesn't just limit lawsuits—it kills them before they start. If you're low-income, that's the whole point. The federal government just institutionalized poverty as a barrier to justice.

Which means, for every challenged provision—from asset tests to asylum rules—it will cost real money and real time to get a day in court. Meanwhile, people will be removed from benefits, blocked from care, and siloed out of democracy. Their legal standing is functionally moot unless they're wealthy, sponsored by NGOs, or backed by corporations. Justice isn't blind—it's blindfolded for the poor.

This chapter doesn't refer to policy tradeoffs or fiscal margin; it's law architecture drawn to resist repeal. It ensures that every aspect of the law—from when it starts to how it ends to how you argue against it—requires an act of congress, a court order, or a bond. That's not a speed bump—it's a moat.

Pragmatically, this turns future policy reversals into televised battles. Want to cancel the wall funding? Say goodbye to federal flexibility and hello to round after round of lawsuits, bonds, injunctions, and interagency paralysis. Want to repair Medicaid standards? Forget it. You'll be defending litigation-ready statutes. Want to update student loan forgiveness? Be prepared for an avalanche of legal defenses and procedural caveats. The inertia isn't by accident—it's designed.

And for those who think politics might self-correct—Congress put it behind the curtain. States, individuals, providers—they may hate the policies. They may lobby. But unless you pass a new law, whatever happens in this bill stands. The burden is on reversal, not regulation. Let the years roll, let enforcement lodge itself, and let statutory permanence take root. That's the bigger strategy.

The legal architecture ends up telling us this isn't a policy—it's a regime. Every clause binds agencies, every sunset limits extension, every enforcement cliff removes discretion, and every plaintiff must carry a bond. And for those with no bonds, no group representation, no institutional backing—that means no challenge. That means no chance. You can't litigate, so you can't resist. That's law by attrition.

If you thought Chapter 18 was about closing the border, this chapter closes the courthouse. Everything here is written to ensure that future damage can't be undone easily. And that's not legislative genius—it's legislative bullying. It weaponizes time, bureaucracy, and courts against democracy.

This is the legal template for a policy to last forever, to resist review, and to fly under the radar until the problems become unfixable. It's structural sabotage wrapped in the veneer of procedural rigor. There's no oversight clause. No emergency reset. No return door. It's not reform. It's foreclosure.

This is how you write a permanent shift—not by winning hearts and minds, but by rewriting the rulebook, shutting down dissent, and pricing the poor out of their right to legal voice. That is chapter 19.

Chapter 20: Tax Benefits Phasing & Limits Remaining

The illusion of generosity evaporates the moment you look past the initial numbers. What appears to be a wave of tax relief is, in practice, a carefully rationed arrangement of conditional benefits that vanish precisely when they might matter most. Income limits, phase-outs, ceilings, cliffs—every mechanism engineered into the code ensures that tax perks do not scale with need, but rather choke off at exactly the point where middle-class families begin to stretch. It's a system built not to distribute equity but to police the edges of eligibility with bureaucratic zeal.

The expanded credits—child, dependent care, education-related deductions—are capped with surgical precision. Take one dollar too much in overtime or freelance earnings, and you trip the phase-out. Suddenly, what was a $2,000 benefit becomes $1,500, then $1,000, and soon enough, nothing. The slope isn't gradual—it's punitive. And it punishes households doing what policymakers love to moralize about: working harder, earning more, building stability. These people are not wealthy. They're not even comfortable. They're simply doing well enough to disqualify themselves from relief designed for them.

Even worse, the phase-outs overlap. You can lose multiple credits at once for the same modest income bump. A two-parent household with three kids and two incomes—teachers, nurses, retail managers—can watch their child tax credit shrink, their dependent care credit vanish, and their earned income credit flatten, all because they nudged into a new bracket. What's the logic? That middle-class success ought to be punished if it isn't perfect.

And don't think itemizing saves you. The SALT cap—still firmly in place—continues to kneecap taxpayers in high-cost states. Property taxes, state income taxes, local levies—all limited to a deduction ceiling so low it may as well be a taunt. The bill extends the high standard deduction and tries to sell it as a simplifier. In reality, it serves as a ceiling that quietly suffocates any attempt by a taxpayer to account for real, regionally inflated costs. New York, California, Massachusetts, and other states with layered tax regimes are treated like anomalies in need of correction. It's not simplification. It's standardization—standardize the pain, especially for people already paying more.

Then there's the mortgage interest deduction—still present, but only to a point. The ceiling remains low, especially for new homebuyers in inflated housing markets. And for those whose homes were financed during the pandemic-era rate dips? Congratulations. You'll get to deduct less of that interest while watching housing costs skyrocket and property taxes remain non-refundable above the cap. For renters, of course, there's nothing—no credit, no deduction, no acknowledgment that housing costs consume more of their income than any mortgage ever did.

Medical expense deductions haven't been expanded. They've barely been maintained. If you don't spend more than 7.5% of your adjusted gross income on out-of-pocket medical costs, you get nothing. No credit for your premiums. No deduction for that ER visit, those out-of-network fees, or your child's therapy sessions. And if you're just unlucky enough to spend 6% of your income—tough. You don't hurt enough to deserve help. The system demands receipts of suffering.

Even charitable deductions—once the gold standard for civic virtue—are corralled. Non-itemizers get almost nothing. Itemizers face limits based on adjusted income. Don't donate more than 60% of your AGI if you want it all to count. And don't expect any thanks for non-cash contributions unless you're meticulously tracking market value appraisals and filing supporting documentation that would make an IRS agent weep. In effect, the government wants your donations, but not your tax deductions.

Meanwhile, investment income retains its advantages. Long-term capital gains remain favored. Dividends enjoy preferential rates. Retirement accounts still shelter the wealthiest effectively. But none of this phases out. None of it cliffs. A billionaire gets the same 20% capital gains rate on millions as a retiree selling $5,000 in mutual funds. There's no means-testing when it comes to investor perks—only for working families.

What the bill has done, with cold efficiency, is draw a tight corridor of benefit eligibility, then pretend that corridor is a thoroughfare. The working poor are too poor to benefit from deductions they don't owe tax on. The upper-middle class makes too much to qualify for phase-limited credits. So what's left? A narrow tranche of taxpayers—usually married, with kids, with employer-provided insurance, living in moderately taxed states—who hit the bullseye. Everyone else drifts outside the margins.

This isn't accidental. It's engineered. The Treasury scores the bill on cost, and lawmakers push benefits to those whose tax profiles keep the short-term expenditure low. A single mother renting in a high-cost city with erratic income? Too volatile. A couple earning $250,000 while paying $30,000 in state and property tax? Too rich. A gig worker toggling between 1099s? Too unpredictable. A salaried couple with stable W-2s, employer-provided insurance, and two kids under 17? Jackpot.

The law codifies these margins. It embeds inequality into the relief. And then it hides behind language like "targeting" and "efficiency." But in practice, these limits are silent punishments. They're how the system avoids spending too much on anyone who might need help continuously or unpredictably. They teach you that the wrong kind of success is failure—and that any deviation from normativity is ineligible for relief.

This approach also guarantees instability. Families can't plan. Tax software can't simplify. Financial advisors guess. Benefits vanish without warning. And every tax season becomes a game of roulette where households don't know what they'll get until they're halfway through their returns.

There are no structural reforms here. No moves toward automatic filing, prepopulated returns, or benefit certainty. Just more variables, more documentation, and more confusion. And it's intentional. Confusion is a cost-saver. If 15% of eligible taxpayers don't claim a benefit, that's a budget victory. If complexity deters low-income filers from itemizing, that's administratively efficient. In the eyes of Congress, silence saves money.

And those who lobby for clearer benefits? They're drowned out by budget hawks with spreadsheet talking points and deficit alarms. It's more politically palatable to cap a deduction than to explain its usefulness. It's easier to kill a tax credit with a phase-out than to fight for its permanence. It's safer to praise "balanced" reform than to admit the structure picks winners and disciplines everyone else.

The system doesn't reward need. It rewards predictability. It doesn't help the struggling. It helps the algorithm-compliant. It's a benefits regime that gives with one hand and claws back with the other—all while blaming the taxpayer for not keeping up.

And when those taxpayers finally sit down, paperwork in hand, to calculate what they're owed, they'll find it's not much. A few hundred here. A shaved thousand there. Less than the cost of rising groceries, rising premiums, rising rent. The benefits are real—but they're structured to feel like ghosts.

That's how this law governs: by tolerating just enough relief to generate applause, and capping it just soon enough to save face. The benefits are publicized. The limits are footnoted. And if your household doesn't match the template? Too bad. You should've read the fine print.

Chapter 21: Clean Energy Credit Rollbacks

The bill doesn't just slice green incentives—it amputates them. What's sold as fiscal housekeeping is actually a surgical strike on clean energy markets and future competitiveness. Tax credits that fueled years of research, deployment, and consumer adoption are all canceled: electric vehicle purchases, home solar installations, clean hydrogen production, charging infrastructure, commercial clean-vehicle programs—gone. Every provision meant to accelerate the transition to a low-carbon economy is erased without ceremony.

This isn't an adjustment, it's a declaration: the clean-energy transition ends now. The federal signal is clear—if you're building a green business, you're burning daylight. Developers racing to launch solar farms or battery factories now face chilling uncertainty. Investors who were calculating returns based on known incentives are abruptly in the dark. Industry players now treat past projections as nostalgia, backward-looking guesses in a market that's just been re-tabulated.

The immediate consequence is predictable—demand dries up. Consumers reconsider EVs when rebates vanish; homeowners defer solar upgrades when rooftop credits evaporate.

Corporations put factory plans on ice. And it's not future pain—it's immediate and quantifiable. Builders cancel projects mid-construction. Factories slow staff hiring. Engineers shift fields. Meanwhile, countries in Europe or Asia accelerate their renewables, while here, the U.S. effectively sends a "Closed for Business" sign to clean-tech talent and capital.

Then comes the drilling doctrine: fossil fuels gain the financial floorboard. Intangible drilling costs, exploration expedition capital, and depreciation perks are reintroduced or expanded. Pipeline income suddenly qualifies for favorable treatment under tax code changes. Big oil and gas playbooks become tax code footnotes. The same structures once reserved for renewables are now redirected wholesale into legacy drilling industries, giving them a cushioned runway in the emerging global energy slump.

The law rewrites regulatory incentives so that if you invest in fossil extraction—or worse, marginal biofuels that meet minimal emissions goals—you get rewarded. Not because it's effective climate policy, but because someone with influence recalibrated the subsidy architecture. This isn't just shifting, it's reallocation: moving money from low-carbon innovation to high-carbon extraction with zero fanfare.

But it gets worse: the definitions are deliberately vague. Clean hydrogen, carbon capture, even battery manufacturing—all get folded into the same taxpayer benefits designed for pipelines. That semantically sanitized disguise allows enormous sums to flow to industries historically barred by emissions frameworks. Fossil-adjacent firms now qualify for "clean energy" rolls simply by adjusting form language. It's carbon laundering through legislative typo.

The strategic timing couldn't be more calculated. After years of green subsidies, lawmakers claim to reprioritize fiscal discipline just as clean tech begins maturity. But the sudden reversal ensures green players get hurt hardest—they made investments backed by policy not sideways promises. Meanwhile, fossil interests get a leg up just when global demand softens and economic sentiment is shaky. They get propped up just in time.

In the broader scheme, this is an economic rerun with catastrophic implications. Regions that planned around green investment—Midwest battery plants, Southeast solar startups, Southwest wind infrastructure—now lose billions in projected growth. Workers trained for EV assembly or clean-grid integration must choose between pivoting to oil rigs or unemployment. Supply chains built around clean innovation contract or dissolve. Equipment manufacturers recalibrate away from solar modules, wind turbines, and electrolyzers. Domestic clean-tech capacity weakens.

Contrary to the law's energy independence framing, this is dependence on fossil continuity—similar to the same extractive engines national security hawks blamed on foreign oil. It's a policy contradiction squared. And while politicians in oil states cheer, communities dependent on green investment are left hollow—not because they failed, but because the rules were ripped out from under them.

We don't pause here. There's no transition buffer—no funding for community job retraining, no port infrastructure for battery exports, no reinvestment in lithium mining or recycling programs. Once the next fossil pipeline or drilling commission is greenlit, the law doesn't fund green workers left behind. Those populations are collateral damage.

Now consider the climate implications. Halting clean energy expansion derails emissions targets instantly. States on track to meet carbon neutrality by 2050 now face recalibration. Grid operators must rebalance demand expectations. Utilities drop renewable obligations and invest in gas peaker plants. Corporate buyers who pledged 100% renewable are forced to renegotiate power purchase agreements—or face greenwashing lawsuits. International credibility erodes: nations don't pivot away from their own climate pledges because one bill did; global coordination falters.

And there's a hidden wrinkle in the seams: once these credits disappear, they're not coming back easily. Green industries sell land, lay off workers, shutter research. Entrepreneurial talent migrates to countries with stable energy policy. Capital moves overseas. Re-enabling the incentives later would require not just political will, but reconstruction—land acquisition, workforce retraining, supply chain reengineering—all at massive cost. Inaction becomes its own echo chamber.

The law isn't a reset button. It's a points system where negative scores compound. Green technology is re-rated as discretionary, non-essential, even impractical. Fossil-fueled extraction is coded essential. Over time, this shapes public perception. The next generation of engineers, financiers, and politicians grow up knowing green policy is unreliable, possibly whimsical. That's cultural collapse, not political compromise.

A final insult: consumer rhetoric is spun around "balance" and "energy independence," but the outcome undermines both. Cleaner energy was the cost-stabilizer. Renewables decoupled grids from volatile oil markets; solar and wind insulated households from fuel spikes. EVs reduced foreign oil dependencies. Now every benefit is withdrawn. Price spikes return. Cost volatility returns. Fossil dependence returns. The public pays the price.

In sum, this rollback isn't energy policy—it's ideological preference hid in fiscal language. It punts on climate responsibility and bets on extraction. It defunds tomorrow's economy and over-funds yesterday's. Those who wanted to see if clean-tech could stand alone got their answer: not under these rules. The transition is over—on paper at least. Meanwhile the carbon bubble grows, regulators stagnate, and the rest of the world speeds past in a green-energized blur.

The consequence is historical drift: Americans will look back and see this as the point where we chose revenue over resilience, extraction over invention, ideology over innovation. We didn't just pause the transition—we reversed it. And that inversion leaves the U.S. playing catch-up with its own destiny.

Chapter 22: Carbon Capture & Clean-Tech Cuts

Funding for climate innovation didn't just shrink—it was surgically targeted, hollowed out, and left to dry. Where carbon capture, advanced batteries, green hydrogen, and semiconductor-scale-up once drew on federal support, this bill has turned the financing tanks to zero. No delays. No transitions. No buffer zones. What remains are empty promises dressed up in ambiguous eligibility language, and zero help for technologies that need it most. Welcome to the rollback lab.

The elimination of carbon capture credits didn't sneak in—it arrived with legislative precision. The provisions once offered to firms installing direct air capture systems, bioenergy with carbon capture, or industrial CO_2 pipelines are nullified. Those credits paid for the heavy lifting—equipment, energy, permitting. Now nothing does. Suddenly, dozens of projects planned or already under construction become financially untenable. Plants in the heartland pivot away from carbon sequestration when the lifeline vanishes. Engineers pivot jobs or leave the industry altogether.

Meanwhile, advanced battery and semiconductor manufacturing were expecting cost-sharing incentives, supply chain subsidies, and production credits. All gone, cut from the bill. The Biden-era policies, aimed at building domestic clean-tech capacity, either never get implemented or get scrapped mid-rollout. The outcome? Lots of shiny factory shells built to U.S. standards that now sit half-equipped, with equipment on hold and workforce training paused. The infrastructure decays standing idle.

Public-private partnerships quickly unravel when federal credit streams dry. Universities lose commitments for clean-tech R&D; tech crowds lose interest; startups that expected matching funds retreat overseas. Private capital flees; venture firms citing "policy uncertainty" green-light foreign solutions. The broken signal is swift: the U.S. is unreliable for climate innovation—don't build here.

You'll hear talk of "budget discipline." That's euphemism for "we don't want to pay a dime." What it means, in practice, is that emerging industries collapse under their own weight. Carbon markets falter. Zero-carbon logistics get second-priority in transportation planning. Instead, existing polluting industries get a financial pad to cover clean investments they're unlikely to make. And imagine the optics: the U.S. spends billions to subsidize fossil-aligned pipelines and drilling rigs, but screws the research that would help phase those out.

Simultaneously, the law offers vague caveats: "limited hydrogen development eligible for some tax treatment," or "geothermal eligible under revamped partnership rules." But they're token-written, legally labyrinthine, and underfunded. They require new regulatory frameworks—and no agency staff, money, or authority. So they slip into the budgetary black hole with no operational capacity for years. In the meantime, tech companies leave or downgrade ambitions, and innovative engineers wind up working for legacy enterprises.

This isn't just about tech. It's about political aspirations. Local governments vote to give permits for carbon sequestration hubs expecting federal dollars they'll never get. They end up scrapping zoning plans, laying off sustainability officers, and tearing down task forces. Community buy-in drains, and the only visible structures are idle, fenced-off concrete pads. Local economies, promised jobs and tax revenue, get left with empty land.

The ripple extends to workforce training. Labor unions, community colleges, and technical programs geared toward clean-tech trades—battery welders, hydrogen plant operators, carbon monitoring specialists—lose curriculum funding. Students looking forward to jobs in clean energy hit hiring freezes. They don't pivot—they pivot away from the field—and the industry pipeline breaks.

Emerging industries need the ladder to scale. The government, from national labs to investment funds, provided that ladder. Without it, many technologies are prisoned in the valley of death—too mature for early grants, too early for commercial loans. The result is obvious: America becomes importer reliant. For green tech, we pay premium for foreign-made batteries and modules—and for carbon capture we outsource the climate problem abroad.

Internationally, the rollback signals are instant. Nations eyeing partnerships or co-development see the U.S. backing out. Companies in Germany or South Korea breathe relief. Investors recalibrate. U.S. clean-tech equities sink. The dollar still buys energy tech—but the dollar no longer funds the innovation.

Let's talk about hydrogen: it was poised to take off in industrial heat, shipping, public transportation, and energy storage. Mere pilot credits existed here, but this bill removes them from mainstream eligibility. States hoping to develop hydrogen hubs lose momentum. Equity investments stall. Import such a hub in five years? Costs will be higher. Jobs will be outsourced. Innovation drought survived on global funding that's now harder to track.

Battery manufacturing was central to EV supply chains and grid storage. There were guarantees of critical mineral refining credits tied to domestic semiconductor-class factories. That funding is zeroed out. Projects in Nevada and Tennessee switched from clean-tech to data centers, or were erased. Clean supply chain aspirations are dismantled mid-build—any new project must now compete globally with China's subsidized manufacturing. Without the offset, they lose.

Then there's the psychological impact: clean-tech entrepreneurs and innovation chairs now have to factor in the U.S. policy risk above engineering risk. That means higher cost of capital, higher expected returns, and less investment in early-stage technologies. It's not Just building bridges tomorrow. It's shutdown of the bridge.

And the myth of the rollback is transparency. They'll call it parity—"we're not picking winners." But here's the truth: you don't need credits to drill holes in the ground. You need them to invent holes in the carbon cycle. The law eliminated the latter while bolstering the former. That's not neutrality—it's hostility.

Now, critics will say markets should decide. But markets follow policy. And private capital flows where government signals reliability. Green energy needs certainty. Fossil fuels don't. Pipelines and rigs last 30–40 years anyway. The capital can't evacuate tomorrow. So the federal code doubles down on existing emissions.

That misalignment compounds climate risk. Every ton of CO_2 that goes underground today is easier to capture and cheaper than addressing it decades hence. Yet the policy steers us away. It retreats from innovations that mitigate carbon when we need them most. That's not progress. It's environmental malpractice.

Even worse: the collapse of public technology sectors removes a cornerstone from national security. If America can't produce its own batteries or hydrogen electrolyzers, it depends on foreign supply chains—even in conflict scenarios. The bill sacrifices resilience in the name of cost-savings that amount to pennies today against dollars lost tomorrow.

Finally, remember that scaling carbon capture, batteries, and hydrogen is a national commitment. There's no wave of private loans ready to fill the gap. Innovation doesn't happen in a vacuum—it happens with government as anchor. That anchor is gone. And until it returns, the United States simply forfeits its chance to win the 21st-century industrial race.

The bill didn't just cut credits. It stopped a strategy. It left a vacuum. And now every clean-tech ecosystem, from R&D to manufacturing to deployment, has to operate without the support it expected and the certainty it needed. That is not fiscal responsibility. It is policy abandonment.

Chapter 23: Clean-Fossil Hybrid Incentives

The law masquerades as a clever fusion of energy policy, but it's nothing more than carbon laundering dressed up as compromise. Instead of choosing a clean path, it amalgamates fossil fuel interests into the veneer of green credibility. Without fanfare, it repurposes "clean fuel" credits to include fossil gas derivatives, and redefines what counts as advanced energy— swapping sustainable promises for hydrocarbon footholds. The result? A legislative Trojan horse, where every mention of 'clean' becomes tainted by corporate profit, and environmental goals are sidelined behind tax loopholes.

At first glance, the language looks innocuous: "clean fuels," "transition fuels," "hybrid energy incentives." But dig deeper and you'll find natural gas syn-gas, methane blends, and even high-emission biofuels slipping into the definition. These are not bridge technologies to a low-carbon future—they're fossil fuel flavors dressed in green. Investors get tax credits—reimbursement on capital costs and grid integration—for projects that meet minimal emissions thresholds. So long as a facility processes fossil gas in a cleaner way than the dirtiest standard, it qualifies. That's not progress. That's stacking the pie with empty promises and smoke-and-mirrors counting.

It gets worse. Carbon capture facilities tied to fossil plants become tax-advantaged, while standalone carbon removal tech is squeezed out. That sends a signal: keep burning gas and retrofit the emissions, don't stop burning. You're telling companies it's easier to stay dirty and offset than to switch to clean innovation. And policies like these are regulatory carrots that re-energize fossil extraction's decay curve, rather than taxing carbon emissions outright. It's a deliberate shove in the wrong direction.

The law even recasts existing public-private infrastructure frameworks—traditionally associated with roads or transit—so they now funnel ramped-up investment into natural gas pipelines and hydrogen hubs based on syngas. Municipalities that thought they were bidding on community energy solutions now find they must adopt fossil-fuel elements to qualify for federal support. The infrastructure is framed as "clean grid resilience," but it's just more pipelines, more compression stations, more environmental risk, and more methane leakage—built under the guise of being 'transition-ready'.

Fuel-cell and hybrid vehicle credits don't escape unscathed. Electric vehicle charging gets de-emphasized while hydrogen blending tanks become eligible for the same credits. That pits emerging clean-tech markets against each other, redirecting capital away from electric networks. The policy pretends to be sector-blind, but it's rigged: it favors incumbents who could retool existing fuel systems at marginal cost. EV owners are left watching as their market priority is downgraded.

R&D hub funding is similarly rerouted. Grant programs once marked for renewable energy now mandate fossil element inclusion. Universities find they must partner with traditional energy companies to qualify. The innovation pipelines morph—not toward sustainable architecture, but toward a just-barely-clean reinterpretation of fossil power. That's not advancing technology. It's bureaucratic reform with environmental slack built-in.

It all funnels into a centralized narrative. Politicians call it a "balanced energy approach." Energy companies call it a lifeline. And communities are told it's about energy independence, domestic production, and grid reliability. But the grid reliability is dependent on assets that erode climate stability. The independence is tied to corporates that export profits overseas. This isn't strategy. It's compromise for compromise's sake.

What about emissions? This is the open loop. Methane venting, fugitive emissions, upstream methane leaks—none of which are accounted for in the incentive thresholds. A facility capturing some CO_2 gets credit, while enough methane leaks to cancel it out. The law works with numbers on paper, not the air we breathe or the climate we burn. If they cared, they'd have caps on upstream emissions. They didn't.

Then comes the public fraud. Energy bills swell for consumers because utilities pass infrastructure costs down. Tax credits go to corporations. Local governments grab applause for attracting energy projects—but forget to mention the environmental liability, emission risks, or community health costs. Those lands transformed under "clean energy investments" still emit particulate, greenhouse gases, and costly degradation.

Worse, this legislation muddies the water for environmental justice. Once-black-and-brown communities are told there's a clean hub coming—until the project includes methane plants or pipeline expansions. Our poorest neighborhoods don't escape unaffected—they're the front lines of "hybrid energy infrastructure," breathing the pollution masquerading as progress.

Taken together, it all amounts to a dangerous mirage: lawmakers count fossil-derived outputs as clean energy and call it a victory. They shift capital into dirty infrastructure while pretending it furthers climate goals. They give credits to the old guard, keep power in legacy hands, and effectively sabotage competition. Meanwhile, real clean technologies either wait for clarity or depart for greener markets overseas.

This isn't compromise. It's capitulation. It suggests that the only way to advance energy policy is through concession to fossil. That if you can't make the system purely green, brown infusion is better than nothing. But in reality, it's worse: it defangs green energy without reducing carbon. It doubles down on extraction rather than supporting decarbonization. It stabilizes the dirty baseline and delays the pivot clean technologies need.

This law doesn't accelerate an energy transition. It plants nails in its tires. And when future generations study why green infrastructure trailed in the critical decades of climate response, they'll look at this moment—this entire policy framework—and see how we rewrote "clean incentives" to support fossil profits and undermine real change.

Chapter 24: Education & Student Loan Overhaul

The bill doesn't reform student debt—it weaponizes administration and shrinks access. What's sold as fiscal responsibility is actually calculated deterrence. The $50,000 cap on graduate borrowing isn't a limit—it's a lockdown. No matter your program cost, you're confined. For many law, med, and pharmacy students, that cap covers tuition but not living expenses. They're forced to either find private loans with higher rates and fewer protections or abandon their career paths altogether. And that's exactly the point: cost containment by exclusion.

Undergraduates feel the squeeze too. Graduate education becomes a two-tier system: those who can self-fund or secure private credit thrive; everyone else is priced out. The bill claims it prevents runaway tuition, but without addressing the root cause—the universities—the result is reduced access, not affordability. Amplify that across public and state-run universities where costs are already high, and you get predictable losses in diversity and capacity. Low-income students and first-generation applicants are the initial casualties of a system built against them.

Loan forgiveness programs are being throttled. Public Service Loan Forgiveness now demands narrower employment qualifications—only specific government or nonprofit roles count. That exclusion hits like a brick on social workers, educators, and community health workers—professions already suffering talent drain. Even if your job counts, the bill tightens terms: stricter documentation, longer employment durations, and fewer qualifying paystubs. If you move between jobs, change employers, or take a short break, your clock resets—straight to zero.

Income-driven repayment plans also get penalized. The guiding principle becomes "pay more for longer." Rigid income thresholds, recertification difficulty, and tighter definitions of disposable income mean borrowers who once qualified for forgiveness now accrue interest and principal for years. A plan designed to adapt to income volatility becomes a bureaucratic death march of paperwork, missed deadlines, and unexpected balance surges. Borrowers are left bewildered, blamed for "not following rules," and branded defaulters by whole numbers rather than circumstances.

The bill layers on accountability for colleges—report graduates' income, debt ratios, and default rates. In theory, transparency protects consumers. In practice, it punishes schools serving nontraditional and underprivileged students. A regional university with high enrollment among first-generation students is at risk, not because it's bad, but because outcomes vary. Worse, financial penalties imposed on low-performing institutions often serve rural or minority communities where capacity is already limited. These schools receive less funding, reduce programs, and sometimes close entirely—shrinking the pipeline into upward mobility even further.

The so-called "value-for-money" framework feels like corporate auditing, but without offering a way out. It's not about improving outcomes—it's about penalizing failure. Those penalties cascade—fewer graduates, less tuition, less research funding, fewer scholarships. The bill shapes a college landscape where only selective, high-earning graduates matter. Everything else erodes.

Student loan servicers are slammed with stricter performance standards. On the surface, that sounds sensible. All borrowers want decent customer service. But there's no funding attached. Servicers must comply anyway, meaning they'll offload employees or cut call-center hours to hit scorecards. Borrowers still face call dropping, lost documents, and misinformation. The system gets more data-driven, less human.

Employer assistance for student loans remains tax-free, but it's optional, not structural. A handful of large employers may cover staff loans, but the bill doesn't require participation or protect lower-wage sectors. Under-resourced employees are still on the hook. America's patchwork employers become the arbiters of who benefits—and most won't play.

The cumulative effect? Borrowers get trapped in debt longer, pay more interest, and lose trust. The student loan system isn't broken—it's being dismantled. And the casualties aren't wealthy college kids—they're mid-career professionals, people of color, rural citizens, and anyone outside the elite.

What's missing is a vision for what comes next. There's no investment in apprenticeship programs, vocational training, or support for nontraditional higher education. No universal grants. No return-to-school stipends. No bridge from college into new apprenticeships. The moment you're locked into debt, no exit ramp is provided. Borrower aid doesn't follow, because the bill assumes fewer eligible borrowers equals taxpayer savings. It's austerity, not strategy.

More perniciously, the student-debt burden shifts quietly away from the government—but only on paper. People still owe. States feel the pressure as school enrollments slide. Universities scramble to justify value. Middle-class home purchases slow. Small-town economies shrink as graduates delay life milestones. That's systemic ripple, not personal consequence.

To call any of this "reform" is misleading. Reform improves outcomes, lowers costs, increases access, and ensures accountability. This bill does the opposite. It restricts enrollment indirectly, penalizes outcomes retroactively, and buries borrowers under complexity. Eligibility becomes rare rather than universal.

The winners are not people—they're balance sheets. The Federal government reduces projected loan costs by kicking them into the indefinite future. Sure, it gains immediate headline savings, but only through borrower failure, not success.

And the political narrative? It's dangerous. Lawmakers can claim fiscal responsibility while the actual policy is to restrict access and reduce forgiveness. They can say "we're saving taxpayers money." They'll hide behind deficit numbers, leaving students to pay the price.

This is not repair. It's predation. Educational opportunity is being dismantled in plain sight, with appeals to accountability and responsibility. But accountability without investment is a sentence for poverty. Responsibility without support is punishment. And reform that shrinks who gets to learn is not policy. It's segregation.

Chapter 25: Immigration & Border Enforcement

There's no nuance here, just a blunt prioritization of prohibition and control disguised as order. The bill resurrects border wall funding with an ironclad mandate: resume construction and don't even think about suspending it later. That's not policy—it's programming. You can't pivot, you can't delay, you can't adapt. It sets an immovable baseline, hacking flexibility out of immigration discourse while installing a permanent barricade that's more ideological than infrastructural.

It's not just the barrier. The bill's surveillance expansion fuels a digital fortress—cameras, drones, sensors, databases—designed to turn the southwestern border into a tech-trapped gauntlet. Every device, every record, every motion detected contributes to a system aimed at surveilling and deterring human movement. It's not about safety. It's about deterrence for deterrence's sake—carved into code and budgeted millions deep.

Then comes the staffing blitz. The number of Border Patrol agents skyrockets. Detention centers lurk behind new hiring. Beds fill new spaces. The system shifts from processing to pause: stop migrations, detain people, hold them indefinitely, or until their legal resources run dry. Speedy deportation trumps due process. And it's intentional. Fewer hearings, fewer lawyers, quicker removals—fulfilling public pressure, not legal standard.

Asylum seekers bear the brunt. New credible fear thresholds don't just raise the bar—they erect it behind razor wire. If you can't immediately and convincingly articulate the trauma that generated your flight, you're denied before you even speak. The bill enshrines transit bans too: pass through a third country without seeking asylum there first, and you're disqualified. It presumes safe passage—regardless of evidence, regardless of situation. That presumes logic and ethics where there is none. It uses geography as a gatekeeper.

The policy doubles down with swift deportation mandates: administratively quick removals without court oversight. Arguments are irrelevant unless filed on paper at capacity. No judicial discretion, no humanitarian latitude. Survival becomes adversarial. Judges matter less than deadlines. Queue time shortens, legal reviews vanish, deportations accelerate. It isn't a functioning system—it's a conveyor belt.

They also add another blow: poles a pause on work authorization. Asylum applicants, who often survive in limbo, now can't legally work until weeks or months later. That legal limbo is financial bankruptcy by design. People who might secure jobs, learn English, or find housing are instead trapped, unsigned, undocumented. The policy ensures desperation while chanting "order restored."

Political theater becomes law with the catch-and-release restrictions. Border agents can't just release migrants with a court date anymore—they must detain them or speed-remove them. That removes discretion completely. There's no room for immigrants with minor infractions, kids with petitions, or families seeking temporary shelter. The system becomes absolute.

What's worse, this bill womanhandles states into the immigration enforcement mesh. State attorneys general can now sue the federal government if it doesn't enforce the law "as written"—meaning any deviation, buffer, or leniency can be litigated at a state level. That bakes conflict into federalism. And it cedes national policy to local politics and partisan grandstanding. If a governor wants stricter removal? They file suit. If another wants leniency? They're blocked. The result? A patchwork of lawsuits and troop deployments that pit states against each other.

To compound it, the bill triggers National Guard activation in border states. Texas, Arizona, California—they can mobilize guard troops without federal sign-off. That militarizes immigration. Civil separation is erased. Migrants face uniformed force, logistics command structures, and threat-of-force oversight—all before any substantive processing has occurred. It's not management—it's deployment design for peace.

Fee hikes on visas, green cards, and work permits complete the cloak-and-dagger: inherent rights now cost more—and costlier processing means bureaucracy slows applicants down so hard that deadlines are missed. Even green-card holders and entrepreneurs feel it. It's not just a barrier to entry; it's a barrier to staying.

Alongside all this, the federal government retreats from humanitarian obligations. Programs for Temporary Protected Status, DACA, and refugee influx quotas are limited or overlooked entirely. Without clarity, they're functionally blocked. It's not intentional cruelty—it's legislative neglect masked as "focus on enforcement."

Then comes the message: "We've fixed the border." Except you haven't. People still cross. They still flee violence. They still need pathways. But now, they face upgraded systems of denial—more walls, more agents, more tech, more detainment, more militarization, and worse—they face legal traps before they have a chance to explain themselves. That's not policy. That's punitive theater.

And this law shrinks the meaningful categories for immigration. Work visas? Costs more, takes longer. Family unification? Slower. Refugee resettlement? Reduced. The entire apparatus pivots away from welcoming complexity and toward enforcing simplicity: no work permits, no asylum, no acceptance. Just rejection.

The real-world consequences echo: local border towns with humanitarian agencies now face stricter constraints. Their volunteers and activists risk enforcement lawsuits. Their funds get redirected. Their ability to provide shelter, legal aid, or crisis management disappears. Migrants flow into gray markets, unregistered, underground, and invisible—without access to basic services, without protection, and without society's oversight. That's not containment. That's displacement.

And don't pretend this isn't calculated. The law doesn't just tighten processes—it weaponizes public emotion. Politicians get the applause now, while future generations inherit the deep-seated costs: litigation, diplomatic friction, labor market disruption, and humanitarian crises. The bill erects no lifecycle for reform—it's designed to persist with no exit.

Worst of all, it's politically immortal. Because hardships are blamed on those who enter illegally, not on the system we created. The populace—even the most charitable—hears "border enforcement," not detention, not denied asylum, not forced deportation. By the time the public realizes it's no longer a system, but a trap, the law has immunized itself behind judicial bonds and political gridlock.

This isn't order. This is ossification. This isn't deterrence. It's displacement. It's not borders maintained. It's borders redesigned—by steel bars, fees, lawsuits, and irony, with enforcement standing on both sides pointing at each other, saying "it's working."

Chapter 26: Detention and Asylum Work Limits

The law doesn't moderate asylum policies—it weaponizes economic deprivation to close the door. By adding a work-authorization freeze for asylum seekers, this legislation removes their ability to support themselves, constraining them into forced dependency or destitution by design. No matter how strong their claim, they are locked out of employment. That isn't compassion. It's coercion.

Imagine fleeing unbearable danger—persecution, violence, starvation—and upon arrival you're turned over to a system that strips you of your ability to work. From that first day, you're told you're not permitted to earn a living legally. You're allowed to stay—but unpaid. You're permitted to exist—but unpaid. That's not justice. It's punishment without conviction.

The policy timeframe matters: delays stretch from weeks to months, sometimes years. Asylum processing capacity is insufficient, legal aid is scarce, and Immigration Courts backlogs are national news. So people sit in limbo. Unable to afford legal representation, housing, transportation, food—yet under threat of detention if they break rules. They survive on goodwill, underground work, or charity. The intent is to drain them economically, making their asylum requests wither from financial attrition, not factual weakness.

Those who do work illegally become fodder for removal. The law's architects count on this: destitution breeds infractions. One wrong move and you're gone. It's a policy loop built on deprivation: punish people until they leave or break the law—then deport them—and claim the system works.

Even those with legitimate safety claims are set up to fail. There are no exceptions for healthcare workers, teachers, or tech professionals. No carve-out for people fleeing recognized peril. You either wait—or you break the rules. Want to help your children get to school? Drive them there? You can't without legal work authorization; you don't have the income or insurance. That's not protection. It's exclusion.

Then there's the chilling effect on community safety. People who want to come forward to report crimes, testify against abusers, or file domestic violence protective orders can't do it without risking deportation or immediate poverty. They stay silent. Without legal work, there's no stability. And silence undermines public safety. The worst part? The law knows it, and still demands compliance. It demands trust in law enforcement but offers no way to legally support that trust. This isn't policy progress—it's calculated disenfranchisement.

For children, the message is brutal: your parents can't work. You are impoverished because you're present. You are penalized for survival. Hunger becomes constant. School attendance fluctuates. Mental health erodes. And none of it is incidental. It's a logical output of the design.

What about humanitarian workers and nonprofits? They're ground-zero responders—providing meals, shelter, legal clinics. They're overwhelmed. The law though, doesn't fund them. It effectively deputizes poverty. Ships of goodwill float into bureaucratic sandbars, starved for resources, shamed for enabling people to live. Charitable organizations become the operational core—but without legal foundation.

The wording? Deceptive. Legislation labels this "work restrictions pending review." Makes it sound passive. Sounds fair. Sound neutral. But in effect, it's starvation by statute.

And let's not overlook the added state-level pressure: States and congressional delegations pouncing on each denial, each delay, each detainment. They rewrite the narrative: it's asylum-seekers who are to blame for their financial failure, not a case backlog or law. Politicians clutch at public frustration. The narrative shifts: "If they just worked, they'd belong." But the law prohibits it. The paradox becomes the propaganda.

Because guilt is easier than grappling with legal complexity. It's easier to scapegoat than to explain that the system intentionally denies work authorization to force departures. It's easier to blame asylum seekers for their own destitution. It's easier to say "the system is too slow," than to admit it's designed to be slow.

And the courts? Here's where it gets darker. The law doesn't just suppress asylum eligibility via work bans—it incentivizes states to litigate federal agencies when work authorization is delayed. It hands state attorneys general standing to sue over agency hesitation. So if Biomédica Clinic waits to provide authorization, a state AG files suit. The courts then freeze agency discretion. A vicious loop: agencies won't clear work permits until legal hurdles are resolved—those hurdles take months. As a result, asylum seekers wait—and fall further behind, financially and socially.

Meanwhile, no oversight is funded to ensure that the federal government upholds minimum service times or improvements. The law mandates deadlines, but strips the budget to meet them. No new staff. No fast-track procedures. No business process re-design. Nothing. In practice, the work prohibition remains indefinite for many.

Let's talk about precedent. The UN Refugee Convention emphasizes that work is essential to empowerment and integration. But this law disconnects protection from participation. You can qualify for asylum, but you can't qualify for work. That removes agency, dignity, and ability to contribute. It's no longer about trajectory—it's about containment.

And don't expect this to just impact recent arrivals. Spouses, kids, mixed-status families—when a parent can't work, they're pushed onto Medicaid costs, school lunch programs, food banks. The burden shifts to states and municipalities, not the federal government. Except there's no state option to address legal limbo. They absorb the human cost, not the policy designers.

The long-term effect is plain: we deter not by building capacity, but by starving possibility. We encourage failure rather than integration. We burn goodwill. We seed mistrust. We create a displaced underclass that avoids courts, avoids police, avoids schools, avoids hospitals—not because they shouldn't, but because the system says "you don't belong yet."

This is immigration policy not at a crossroads, but in retreat. Enforcement becomes a barricade, not an endpoint. Work becomes a punishment, not a right. Detainment becomes the default, not the exception. Humanity becomes an irr. And suffering becomes a policy lever.

If lawmakers want to restrict migration, do it honestly and humanely. But this? This is moral obfuscation. It hides cruelty in paperwork, responsibility in adjudication. It punishes people for things they can't control and expects them to pay in hardship—and for that punishment to be called legal policy. That's not reform. It's control by deprivation. And at best, it's legacy for our generation's suffering.

Chapter 27: Implementation Timelines & Sunset Clauses

The law's architects didn't just program policy—they set a time bomb. Most major changes kick in January□1,□2026. Medicaid and SNAP shifts stagger through 2027–2028. Student loan restructuring syncs with the next academic cycle. These staggered starts aren't benign—they're strategic delays that defuse public outcry while ensuring reversals evaporate before people notice.

Sunset clauses litter the text like land mines: senior tax benefits, Trump accounts, Medicaid expansions—they self-destruct after five years unless reauthorized. That's political insurance masquerading as fiscal restraint. Except no one actually expects Congress to revisit them. Predictably, we'll hit the cliff just before an election, with everyone calling suspensions "temporary," then shrugging once the clock runs out.

But the kicker is less obvious: midstream deadlines are weaponized. Agencies are required to implement rules by specific dates, but they're given no funding, staff, or system upgrades. They either meet the deadlines or violate the law—putting them squarely in legal crosshairs. If a department delays, it's sued. No extensions. No emergencies. No leniency. Instead of empowering agencies to reply by intent, the law forces them to comply by threat.

Consider a hurricane hitting in September□2027. SNAP eligibility rules for that year automatically adjust, even if state offices are destroyed. Agencies have no leeway to pause—so they either print guidance from ashes or face litigation. That isn't oversight. It's tyranny coded into law.

Sunsets can also be Trojan horses. A benefit enters the statute with five-year life, but layered within is a provision that "may be extended by Congress." That means the benefit can stay forever—with no requirement it be reviewed or reevaluated. Want repeal? Good luck dragging lawmakers to the floor on something that's always marked "optional." It's permanence hidden as temporariness.

Then there's the silent escalator. Some programs sunset automatically unless funding is approved. But others reverse by default—childcare credits don't expire until after next election, while some green energy incentives disappear in one tax cycle. What looks like symmetry is chaos. Implementation calendars diverge, priorities vanish, protections unravel unpredictably.

On the political timeline, everything is engineered to avoid accountability. Politicians get bragging rights in the early years—"We locked it in!"—while the unwind happens behind the scenes when they're off the ballot. Consumers won't connect the drop in benefits to the law—they'll just feel costs rise and call it inflation-borne.

This also sows legal chaos. Providers who expanded Medicaid programs in 2026 can't predict if their funding stays in 2029. They hire staff based on federal comfort, only to get cut interim due to sunset language few track. They're left with stranded assets and rehiring costs. Patients lose taken-for-granted services.

The real power play: sunsets mean no one's responsible, but everyone benefits while clocks are running. By the time reversals matter, lawmakers shift blame to agency deadlines, fiscal constraints, or "temporary sacrifices for long-term balance." It's classic policy camouflage.

Worse still, sunsets are news-sinkholes. Yesterday's five-year benefit cutoff barely makes it past the scroll. No public campaign covers it. No mass awareness. No outrage. It disappears, quietly and permanently, under the radar of people who never received the memo.

In effect, the legislation builds a façade of generous but temporary support—before cratering it with built-in timers. Everyone feels the relief, nobody experiences the withdrawal. By 2030, benefits vanish, access shrinks, and the public is told it's for the budget. The timing is perfect—after credit, before contempt.

This is policy Ponzi. You recruit with promise, but funding circularities and statutory clocks collapse. No collapse—just expiration. No scandal—just absence. And by the time people ask what happened, there's no roll-back vote to point to, just a silent layer of line items that disappeared.

That's how you lock in advantage without owning it. You give just enough time for compliance, adoption, dependency, and political credit—and then, when no one's looking, you revoke it. And because no one tracks sunsets, few cry foul. That's bureaucratic euthanasia, not policy evolution.

Chapter 28: Restricted Agency Flexibility

Congress didn't just rework policies—it cut the nerve endings of our administrative state. This chapter nukes any ability federal agencies had to adjust, interpret, or freeze provisions. What's sold as "rigorous compliance" is actually a strategy to cripple adaptive governance. Agencies like IRS, HHS, and Education are given binding interpretation mandates—with lawsuits and enforcement by states or individuals hanging over every decision. No flexibility. No mercy. No grey area. Policy is now a brick wall.

Regulatory drift is gone. If a clause says "effective Jan 1, 2026," the agencies have to enforce it. No delays. No deadline shifts. Even during emergencies. Customer service? Too bad. Natural disasters? Too bad. System crashes? Too bad. If guidance isn't released on time, if exemptions aren't provided when reasonable, if administrative complexity overwhelms constituents—the law doesn't care. Step one of implementation? A legal minefield.

Agencies must read and apply text, not theory. Precedent doesn't matter. Intent doesn't matter. Courts now analyze whether agencies followed literal wording. Take the Thrifty Food Plan freeze: if USDA decides inflation triggers an update before 2027, states or citizens can sue—with bond requirements attached. The policy shift inadvertently ties bureaucrats' hands while emboldening legal challengers.

Politically, that's the point. Elected lawmakers draft legislation knowing agencies won't tweak it later. Want to retract benefit amounts mid-crisis? Too bad. Want to adjust income thresholds in face of recession or pandemic? No. Temporary overrides are banned. The rulebook is immutable, and agency-led fine-tuning is banished. That effectively moves administrative power from agencies to courts—and to Congress itself.

This isn't theoretical. It rewrote HHS expenses in 2028. Administrative discretion for Medicaid redeterminations during emergency orders? Gone. Any agency memo that conflicts with letter of law can trigger an immediate injunction forcing them into court. Services halt. Institutions scramble. Citizens suffer. Enforcers win.

To amplify the damage, states and individuals now have standing to sue for non-enforcement. If HHS fails to change a Medicaid application deadline after a hurricane, a state AG or nonprofit lawyer can file suit. They can compel adherence to text—or seek a judicial stay. Agencies are trapped: follow law and ignore practicality, or delay and get sued. Neither route serves public need.

This applies to all domains: immigration waivers, tax implementation guidance, SNAP eligibility rulings, student loan servicer standards. Each needs accurate, timely guidance, but now agencies must choose between practicality and liability. The result? Conservative default. Instead of innovating or relaxing rules, agencies issue memos titled "Delay forthcoming guidance." That's inertia by fear.

The law doesn't just discourage flexibility—it punishes it. If you launch a pilot without court validation, you're vulnerable. If an agency verbally reassures a stakeholder about filing timelines, you can be sued. Every briefing memo is a policy shackle. Staff live in constant fear: one slip-up, and they're in court.

That fear tanks agency morale. Compliance officers demand top-down sign-offs. FOIA requests spike. Each meeting notes down every nuance, because nuance might be witness. Bureaucracy becomes safeguard-first. No chance-taking. No adaptation. Innovative programs die before pilot funding is secured.

What does this mean for the public? Canned responses. One-size-fits-all forms. No soup-for-you exceptions. A family with a missing social security document can't get help until their entire application matches exact definitions—even in crisis. What's legal is all that matters. And if what's legal is insufficient? Too bad.

Meanwhile, lawsuits flood both ends. Some groups sue to force enforcement—"why aren't you enforcing clean energy credits word for word?" Others sue to stop enforcement—"your Medicaid recertifications are overdue." Agencies lose flexibility and face legal whiplash from both sides. Even states fight states: red or blue, all armed with the same tools. Judicial bandwidth is overwritten with regulatory compliance cases.

This doesn't just kill flexibility—it restructures federalism. Congress votes the law. Judiciary enforces literalism. Agencies get blamed for chaos. But Congress retains political cover—they passed the "fix." Judges are de facto rule-enforcers.

Lawyers become policy administrators. Not one thing became more accessible. Everything became legally at risk.

By shrinking agency discretion, the law transfers real power: from public service to politicized litigation. Want change? File a suit. Want delay? File a suit. Want funding? Wait for an act of Congress. Regulatory updates? Not allowed. Meanwhile, policy surfaces show static façades, but underneath the machinery shudders.

The philosophy is clear: we don't trust agencies, we don't trust emergencies, we don't trust public need. We trust courts, lawyers, bond-backed suits, and hired congressional staff with their spreadsheets. That's not democracy in practice. That's policy by paralysis.

The worst part? No provision requires periodic review of the rigidity. Once agencies are pinned, Congress doesn't revisit the structural freeze. There's no sunset on literalism. No pilot to test whether flexibility helps. No escapes from the freeze. The policy remains hyper-literal until repeal—which is politically unlikely. The law becomes doctrinally recursive.

Citizens caught in the web? They won't know until they need help. Their benefits get hung up on missing semicolons in statutes. Their tax rebates rejected because the agency delayed a memo by a week. Their public service forgiveness resets because the loan servicer used the old paperwork. Their asylum cases dismissed because of a form not yet updated. The message: we invert the policy paradigm to where assistance is suspended until conditions are perfect, rather than provided until wrongdoing is proven.

That's code-defined austerity. It's "policy by default." And it ensures that no future administration—not blue, not red—can fix glitches without legal obstacles. We've frozen the system in place, locked, loaded, and legally prosecutable. Complexity isn't an accident—it's the result. Agencies can't operate. People can't qualify. Chaos is baked in while responsibility is shoved outward.

In sum: flexibility isn't optional—it's illegal. Pragmatism is a lawsuit waiting to happen. Compassion is secondary paperwork. And the policy principle remains: hard lines beat human need. Because once public service becomes a legal liability, bureaucracy becomes a defensive wall—and the people are left outside.

Chapter 29: Legal Bond Barrier

Nothing strains access to justice like slapping a price tag on it—and this law does exactly that. A new bond requirement now stands between every citizen and federal court relief. A legal bond—posted before even a preliminary injunction—is required if you challenge anything in this bill. No bond means no case. It turns the courts into gated fortresses, accessible only to those with wallets, not valid claims.

This isn't neutral policy—it's hostile architecture for legal combat. Too poor to post a bond? You automatically lose. Your rights, state benefits, agency errors—none of it matters if you can't pony up collateral upfront. We told judges to interpret law strictly; now we tell litigants to buy the right to be heard. Justice, it seems, is a privilege for the wealthy.

The bond amounts? Calculated for maximum deterrence. Agencies request bonds that cripple challengers before challenge even begins. Families affected by SNAP, workers in wrongful ICE detainment, adults locked out of Medicaid, students robbed by loan servicer failure—they all face the same barrier. Their lived injustices remain unresolved because a judge can't even evaluate their case.

Organizations can band together, but class-action suits run into bond requirements too. Want to represent 1,000 clients? Post a bond covering estimated agency costs, court expenses, even potential financial harm. That means nonprofits and legal aid groups—already underfunded—will likely refuse to take smeary cases they can't pay for.

What happens to small lawsuits? They vanish. No weekend worker fighting wage theft. No single mom demanding overdue benefits. No asylum seeker pushing back on expedited removal. No student defrauded by school loan processing. The smallest claims vanish as if they never existed. Courts are cleared of clutter. But not because complaints weren't valid—they just couldn't afford the entry fee.

There's no exemption. Public-interest litigators aren't immune. Community-based legal services are not exempt. Challengers from "low-income" aren't protected. We're not talking about opposing multimillion-dollar corporations. We're diagnosing that the legal system has become economically gated. Only those with financial means can ask a judge: "Were rights violated?"

The law also installs a fatal chill: attorneys won't touch cases where clients can't afford bonds. That shrinks representation.

The logic is simple: no bond, no fee; no fee, no case. No case, no challenge. Legal suppression by ordinance.

What's more, bond hearings themselves waste valuable time—time claimants don't have. A bond is usually required within days of filing. That triggers emergency motions, hearings, travel, legal fees—before anyone even considers the merits. Then the agency can drag it out. Bonds can be raised, reduced, appealed—but meanwhile, the case stalls, and the law stands unchallenged. It's a strategic delay mechanism.

Imagine if, after a health crisis, courts require bond to challenge medication pricing. Or if schools demand a bond before any disability discrimination suit. Health clinics drained. Consumer advocates retreat. Media watchdogs dissociate. That's what's been institutionalized here, focused squarely on benefits and civil rights—but easily adaptable.

Public agencies can still file bonds. Corporations can litigate with impunity. Only the powerless pay to speak.

There's no "public interest" carve-out. No sliding scale tied to citizenship status. No judicial oversight to waive the rule. It's systemic and complete. Legislators call it "deterrence," but critics call it "civil disenfranchisement."

The net effect is instant: fewer lawsuits, fewer injunctions, fewer agency reversals. That's good for project timelines, policy continuity, and fiscal forecasting. It's even good for conservative legal wins. But it's disastrous for transparency and accountability.

Remember, the courts aren't only for enforcement—they're for protection. Rights aren't preserved through votes—they're preserved through challenges. And when the barrier to challenge is a bond, rights lose, not politicians.

The bond barrier doesn't hide behind rhetoric. Its effect is immediate. Families who'd apply for expedited SNAP reinstatement can't. A student who can't afford bond loses momentum and debt piles. If an immigrant is wrongly detained, no court hears it fast enough. Agencies are freed from coercive oversight. Enforcers are emboldened. Citizens are powerless.

This bond requirement stands as a policy executioner. Not by public consensus. Not by clear law. But by economic gatekeeping. And while a few might dig into grants or donations to fund challenges, the majority are left without recourse.

Future lawmakers will talk about judicial restraint and "backlog reduction." But what's really happening is rights being squeezed out. Access to courts has become a market good: line up in cash or stay silent. And that's not democracy—it's monetized justice.

If you wonder why agency excess goes unchecked, here's why: the system removed the tools for accountability. You can't challenge assignment of Medicaid redetermination. You can't sue for student loan mishandling. You can't contest denial of asylum or enforce bond bonds back. Every challenge demands capital. And most people don't have it.

Chapter 30: Longevity by Legal Rigidity

This bill doesn't just rewrite policy—it cements it with legal mortar. Every provision, every cap, every restriction is packaged inside unyielding legislative language. The result: a labyrinth of statutory precision crafted not to be understood, but to be unchangeable. It's not law meant for governance. It's law built to outlast need.

Here's the mechanism: The bill's text isn't approximate. It's exact. It doesn't say "agencies may consider," or "in emergencies." It says "shall," "must," and "no discretion." That's not style. It's resistance engineering. That's how you bake in longevity. Once etched, the only way to shift it again is precisely the same act of political violence—replacing the entire statute. Not re-regulate. Rewrite.

Sunset clauses? Rare. Most chapters, once inserted, remain indefinitely. Even those rare five-year timers? They're designed to die without notice. No reporting requirement, no public review. One line of text removes your benefit silently and permanently. No repeal votes, no agency memos, nothing necessary but not action.

The rigidity applies across all sectors: tax, health, education, immigration, energy. Nothing is modular, nothing is agile. You cannot tweak income thresholds to match inflation. You cannot adjust work exemptions for SNAP in crisis. You cannot change student loan forgiveness metrics as economic conditions shift. There's no built-in fail-safe, no automatic update clause, no waiver system. Change isn't optional. Change is hostage.

The bill forbids regulatory flexibility. Agencies cannot issue temporary orders. They cannot create emergency patches. Even in war or disaster, the law must be enforced exactly as written. Want to extend Medicaid enrollment during a hurricane? Not allowed. Want to delay tax payments in a recession? Not allowed. Want to pause deportations for pandemic safety? You can try — but the law will cut you off mid-attempt and you could be sued, by a state, a corporation, or a sovereign individual.

Most bureaucracies expect leeway. They build flex into their budgets, staff schedules, contingency plans. This law starves them of it. Staffers who invented workaround guidance for pandemic chaos now live in legal terror. Every line in analysis memos is tagged with warnings. Get one wrong phrase and a state AG fires a suit that blocks your entire agency. That isn't adaptability. That's paralysis by prescription.

Even democratically accountable actions—like agency petitions to Congress—are undermined. You can ask. You can lobby. You can testify. But until lawmaker votes flip or text changes, you can't execute. That's legislative permanence disguised as efficient regulation. It's a veneer of decisiveness masking systemic crippling.

From a game-theory perspective, it's a Hobson's choice: accept policy rigidity or risk court backlash. Constraints are absolute, discretion is zero. That's how the bill outmaneuvers future administrations. No amount of executive orders can pause, transpose, or reverse structural policy anchors—they violate the letter of the code. Court challenges will stall implementation and saddle agencies with punitive litigation. That's the mathematical gamble: agencies will not enforce anything not explicitly ordered—even if it kills people.

Corporations? They benefit. Because anarchic regulation becomes immaterial when it's easy to say, "We followed the statute." Want to dispute deferred implementation? They accuse agencies of activist overreach. Want to maintain fossil-fuel credits? They cite "shall" clauses. Want to tighten immigration screening or Medicaid redetermination? They simply affirm agencies followed procedure. It's veto power by statute.

Agencies can't issue clarifying executive rulings. They can't adjust forms. They can't shift deadlines. They can't issue reporting extensions. They only have two options: obey or be sued. The risk is real. Every deputy secretary is now under threat of removal at lawsuit loss, bond requirement, or judicial stay.

That's how the law achieves longevity: not with supporters, but with weaponized rigidity. The system breeds inertia. Policy becomes unassailable—until political coalitions shift enough to override. And override isn't easy. It's replacing a statute meant to suppress flexibility.

This design is surgical. It doesn't draw attention. It doesn't broadcast permanence. It's a soft tyranny. But the impact is cumulative. SNAP thresholds never adjust. Clean energy credits never return. Medicaid waivers never reappear. Immigration rules never loosen. Courts remain dormant. Agencies wait for signals that never arrive.

Future political swings won't matter. The memo "can't implement" will read the same in any administration. The court will say "text forbids it." The judge will call it "legally binding." The language is king—and language never forgets. It outlives its architects.

The true permanence isn't in ideology—it's in architectural text. The bill isn't about content change, it's about structural resilience. It creates legal scaffolding built to resist decay and adaptation. It chooses rigidity over remedy. That's how policy becomes doctrine—and doctrine becomes default.

Look beyond votes. Look at the language. That's where longevity lives. The law won't be repealed by budget compromise or rhetorical shift. It will only be chipped away by another act of code. Which is possible—but remotely so. You can campaign. You can litigate. You can lobby. But until the law is rewritten, its text remains both anchor and chain, quietly shaping public life for decades to come.

That's what longevity by legal rigidity means. It's the silent permanence of policy—locked into place, unresponsive, unyielding. And unless future lawmakers recognize its structural weight, they'll keep living under its unspoken iron logic.

Chapter 31: Everyday Impact Snapshot

Start with this: the bill isn't theoretical or bureaucratic. It's real. It's you, your neighbors, your family, your paycheck. All those policy changes colliding in living rooms, at checkouts, in hospital waiting rooms, in crowded classrooms. We've unpacked how each section works—but here we show you what it actually looks like when legislation meets human life. No abstraction. No summaries. No fluff. Just the lived damage or gains.

Picture the working family in a small town: two adults, three kids. Taxes? They benefitted briefly from a child credit that disappeared six months ago, but income phase-outs gutted other benefits. Their household income hovers just below the cliff—one raise and they lose half the credits. So they reject overtime. That choice saves them from losing benefits, but costs thousands. A textbook case: the bill handed them an illusion of help and then forced them to choose stagnation over advancement.

Imagine the grandmother in rural Appalachia managing her Medicaid. She ages in place, keeping costs down for everyone. But under new rules, her home equity now counts, her paperwork must be refilled quarterly, and a single missed deadline means a coverage gap. She calls for help. State staff—underfunded, tired—can't respond until next week. In the meantime, she skips medication refills. That's not policy. That's life-threatening red tape.

Then consider the graduate student at a state university, aspiring to a PhD in public policy. The $50k loan cap means her entire tuition—never mind living expenses—is only partially covered. She looks into private loans, but the interest rate, variable with no forgiveness, stacks so high it could take her lifetime. She either gives up the program or takes on systemic debt. Either way, her plans die.

Now look at the rural electric co-op in the Midwest. They planned for solar array funding, batched batteries, EV charging stalls. Their grant was canceled. Cost estimates doubled. They shelved the infrastructure. A few months later, their neighbor town in Canada installs a grid battery that stabilizes energy costs. The co-op? They get stuck with coal-volatile pricing. Their budget? Blown up for a failure that began in Congress.

Consider the restaurant worker earning tips and relying on overtime. For one paycheck, tips aren't taxed. For another, they disappear under phase-outs. For overtime, it's tax-free—until their wage push them out. The unpredictable income pattern—normal for the sector—becomes a tax roller coaster. Each month they worry: will I owe or will I get? And what do I do if I owe while back-paying on a capped debt payment schedule? They tip-toe around work. Their take-home pay declines. They can't plan how to pay rent or bills. And that's before an emergency hits.

Then there's the single mom in a mixed-status household. She receives partially prorated SNAP, but now her teenage son's undocumented uncle's income is counted. They struggle with deductions lost when her utilities rise past eligibility cut-offs. Internet isn't included, so she loses access to remote job resources. Her children's homework is compromised; her part-time remote work falters. Nothing was done consciously. Everything was foreseen.

Imagine the newly arrived asylum-seeker with a valid claim, living in provisional housing. He cannot work and cannot earn money. He waits in limbo for months, while living costs drain savings. He attends ESL classes—until he can't afford the fare. He's discouraged. He's a future teacher, a cultural contributor.

Instead, he becomes a burden. And then he becomes an illegal worker—low paid—no benefits—vulnerable. That's exactly where the policy positions him.

What about energy engineers in Tennessee? Atmospheric scientists in Arizona? Battery researchers in Colorado? Their jobs dried up. Their projects were canceled. The companies folded or relocated production overseas. Those specialized workers relocated, changed industries, or left the field. That intellectual capital hourglass now drains time, funding, and talent away from the U.S.

Across the border, small-town nonprofits don't survive. Organizations essential to community health—food banks, legal clinics, health coalition groups—lose funding tied to SNAP or Medicaid outreach. Obesity prevention, diabetes programs—they lose credibility and donations. People suffer silent illnesses. Healthcare deserts widen. Hospitals feel it in uncompensated care costs; counties write off deficits. It adds up in property taxes. It kills quietly.

Working families with children needing childcare soak up dependent-care credits. That credit gets hit—they qualify for half of what they expected. Their employer-based childcare subsidy is phased out due to income bump. They're priced out of childcare entirely. One parent quits working. Household income drops. New benefit eligibility doesn't kick in. They have no buffer, no backup—just the policy's cold math.

Rural hospitals? They lose Medicaid reimbursements because of tightened rules. Rural seniors need nursing home care but can't qualify because home equity limits rose. Those homes become a jail—not a refuge. Families scramble to cover care out-of-pocket. They either move grandparents, bankrupt themselves, or let care collapse. It's happening quietly across thousands of counties.

Employees at a farm can't qualify for work-dependent SNAP anymore. Utilities go up in winter. They lose benefit recalculation due to frozen deductions. They cut back grocery budget. School-age children lose concentration. They spend lunch money on energy. The state agency? Still union-driven and understaffed. They miss deadlines. Appeals fail because cases are backlogged beyond the allowed 30 days. People are cut.

Tax accountants now advise "don't go after credits" because benefits fall off the cliff too fast. Freelancers restructure their income. Lawyers shield their employees' overtime. For many, this becomes a tax optimization exercise not for advantage, but for preservation. That reflects a broader change: do less and stay poorer, because higher wages cost us relief.

Communities planning green energy hubs? Developers cancel solar arrays. EV charging contracts freeze. Battery deployment postponed. Local sales taxes underdeliver. Streetlights stay old. Grid parity doesn't happen. Residents pay more in utility bills. The money promised by the federal code drained away at legislative blackboard. And no authority can fix it. Pipeline energy gets funded instead—visible, brutal, fossil-fueled infrastructure.

A college student confused by indecipherable paperwork quits halfway through her loan recertification window, missing the deadline by two days. Her loans snap back to full interest status. Her payments double. She drops out after one semester. She's a casualty. Documentation failure—not missing tuition—is the cause. She's told she "should have read fine print." That's policy in action.

Even when the policy delivers real benefit—like the senior deduction or tip and overtime exclusions—it falls short of meaningful change. The dollars are overshadowed by rising housing costs, medical prices, utility spikes. Those benefits are patching holes, not building roofs. She gets $600 a year but pays $3,000 more in insurance premiums. He gets $400 credit, but utilities cost $2,000 more annually.

That's what everyday impact looks like: marginal wins bleeding into larger losses in the cumulative ledger of one life. Single benefits against rising costs don't balance—especially when the system penalizes progress. The law guarantees unpredictability, complexity, and injustice. Every support comes with a precision-cut knife at its edge.

Don't paint this as abstract policy. It's microchips of legislation lodged in the lungs, kidneys, bank accounts, education pathways, work ethic, mental health, family decisions, and life plans of millions. The bill is that personal. And until we see it that way—through lived stories—we'll keep debating it like another ideological checkbox. But the ripple of every clause moves through dinner tables. And it's these ripples that define real time: real people waking up hoping things don't get worse—and waking up each day finding they might.

Chapter 32: Winners, Losers, and Trade-Offs

This isn't about neat outcomes or balanced budgets. It's a deliberately constructed scoreboard—one where the winners are written into law, and the losers are collateral burnt. Every provision favors someone, explicitly or structurally, but every victory is someone else's wound. Underneath the veneer of policy trade-offs lies a design of winners, losers, and calculated sacrifice.

First and foremost, the "middle" earners—two-income professional couples with kids, employer-provided benefits, and incomes just below the cutoff—win. Their tax returns receive modest boosts: child credits, senior exemptions, tip and overtime shields. They're the demographic sweet spot the law targets. In return, they shoulder stability expectations: no raise, no extra income. They win enough, but not too much, and get enough relief without asking for more.

Fossil fuel corporations ride a separate wave. The law breaks no ground for renewables, but it gives greens lights for fossil innovation cloaked in tax subterfuge: pipeline depreciation; intangible drilling credits; methane loopholes. If you're Chevron, Exxon, a pipeline operator, or an industrial gas manufacturer, congratulations—you received a renewed playbook, unchallenged tax incentives, and implicit subsidy. The law doubles as fossil energy policy by omission of climate urgency.

Also winning are legal lobbyists and bond-exploitant law firms. When legal bonds gate courts, only those with deep pockets—corporate plaintiffs, defense contractors, and bureaucracies—can litigate. Bond requirements ensure the legal playing field tilts, protecting agencies and industries but burying low-income plaintiffs in legal fees. Public-interest advocates see their caseload dry up, while corporate lawyers feast.

Student loan servicers—whether private companies or banks servicing federal debt—bless the tightening of forgiveness. More borrowers grind interest, miss deadlines, escalate balance rather than purge it. Revenue flows inward. Complaints fall as paperwork grows. The industry gains a tether to income, not relief.

Hourly workers with unpredictable income patterns lose. The promise of tax-free tips and overtime evaporates for many once they hit thresholds. Their net income becomes a rationed fringe. People working double shifts pass a cliff and become worse off, not better. The law convinces them to stop trying—"don't earn more, or lose it all."

Aspiring professionals—graduate students, PhD candidates, those in advanced study fields—are boxed out. The $50,000 debt cap doesn't just limit options; it charts futures. They lose premium careers, leaving rural states and public universities empty. Diversity exits. Gatekeeping enters.

Mixed-status and immigrant families lose net traction. SNAP income-counting rules, work caps, and eligibility freezes erode household stability. Remember, the undocumented uncle or cousin now stiffens the entire household's calculation. The family eats less, sleeps more tentatively, drops extracurriculars. The result: hardship becomes policy.

Seniors in fixed-income situations lose. The senior deduction phases out quickly. Their home equity counts against them. They get Medicaid redetermination more often. Nursing homes remain understaffed. Medicare savings stuck in moratorium cliffs. Their support is present—but deliberately narrow, hanging on precise definitions that erode by inflation and bureaucracy.

Under-resourced states lose. When administrative cost-sharing plummets from 50% to 25%, or SNAP error-penalty clauses hit, those states hemorrhage staff and efficiency—and pass cuts onto citizens. Rural counties see hospitals go under, public transit decline, school meals delayed. Local tax bases buckle. Rural poverty deepens while federal policy takes credit.

Clean energy advocates and workers lose twice. First when green tax credits vanish. Again when carbon capture allowances shrink. Investments shift overseas. Clean energy hubs collapse. Workers retrain out of green trades. Startups pivot to other industries. America loses global competitiveness.

We're told it's trade-off politics. But what trade-offs? Which costs are acceptable? This law avoids asking those tough questions. The price of austerity is poverty, the cost of certainty is injustice. The narrative is that trade-offs preserve popularity and protect the fiscally prudent. The reality: trade-offs enforce inequality, freeze opportunity, and reward old money and entrenched interests.

There's no consideration for long-term climate, educational outcomes, or safety nets. There's no sliding scale or future track padding. Instead, all choices favor immediate fiscal optics over future resilience. We swapped creativity for control. We exchanged human dynamism for policy certitude. And we accepted that some demographic could fill the void.

The bill sells itself as technocratic. Complex tables, sliding curves, sunset clauses. A policy toolbox that "lets data decide." But data is only rubber-stamped into codified control. There is no flexibility to use data. Agencies can't adjust. Courts can't pause exigency. Structures freeze.

Making policy "technical" doesn't hide political intent—it reinforces it. Because it tells people "you can't change this." By embedding a seemingly neutral structure, lawmakers make revolt difficult. We won't debate. We'll comply. And if a tool becomes a weapon? Too bad.

Unlike budget cuts that lawmakers can restore, these provisions entrench disadvantage. A student who can't take a graduate program due to debt cap isn't going to wait five years for reauthorization. An immigrant parent stuck in asylum limbo isn't going to remember to apply again centuries later. A battery factory that shuttered doesn't reopen if climate incentives return. These losses are quick, brutal, and permanent.

We're told you can't grow the economy, educate everyone, stabilize healthcare, fight climate change, and keep budgets balanced. This law leans hard into those "you can't have it all" politics—but does so by choosing winners based on privilege, not need. The moral failure is in the equation: justice is assumed unaffordable unless trimmed by deprivation.

Health. Independence. Mobility. Opportunity. Potential. Responsibility has become another way to say "burden on taxpayers." So people stop trying to teach, invent, mother, risk, or help. Every citizen now weighs an opportunity against a formula: will I break the system if I get better? And if the answer is yes—then middle-class stasis becomes the new American dream.

If you're a winner today—congratulations, you've succeeded under the bill's narrow conditions. But winners never reform systems. They reinforce them. If you're a loser—child, immigrant, rural homeowner, student, worker—you're trapped in the bill's architecture. These damage points accumulate by section. That's how policy becomes generational.

What's left for society? Either dig in and revise the architecture—or withdraw. Reform won't come from political steam. It must come from moral reckoning. Because depending on legislative versions that can be rewritten? You'll just be picking winners again. We've been there before.

Chapter 33: Equity and Access Concerns

Let's call it what it is: this legislation doesn't fix inequality—it amplifies it. It weaponizes bureaucracy, not biology. It erects walls under the guise of efficiency. Where it claims to promote fairness, it enshrines fragility. "Equity" becomes synonymous with "exception made for a few"—not systemic inclusion. Complexity, not compassion, becomes the gatekeeper. This isn't reform. It's a rebrand of exclusion.

Mixed-Status Families: Surveillance, Not Support
If you live paycheck to paycheck in a household where not every member has legal status, congratulations—you're now under financial surveillance. The minute Uncle José, here on a temporary visa, earns a few hundred dollars, your SNAP or Medicaid benefits shrink. His income counts against the whole family, even though he's technically ineligible. This law doesn't separate contributions from eligibility—it conflates them. It treats immigrant households not as communities, but as calculators. One small job? That's a subtraction from food you can feed your kids. That's equity? No. That's eviction by budget.

Small-Town Agencies on the Chopping Block
In cities with lawyers, case managers, translators, and infrastructure, bureaucracies will limp on. In towns with county clerks pulled between animal control and transit, you're left waiting. States must hit error-rate thresholds or lose funding. After the cut, they freeze hiring. Staff exits under budget stress while case files pile up. Who loses? The rural grandmother who can't refill her prescription in time, or the family who waits six months for student loan deferment. That's a disparity baked into text.

Gig Economy Grief: Work Becomes Liability
If you think your side hustle is a safety net, think again. Independent contractors already juggle unpredictable income. Now, any small spike can tip them out of earned-income credits or tax deductions. One good month becomes a

penalty. The system elicits stability through detours, not support. You can't fix volatility by punishing variability. You just push entrepreneurs away—from innovation, from flexibility, from tomorrow.

Renters Bear the Invisible Burden
The logic is inverted: home equity grows old citizens out of coverage; renters—who often pay more monthly—get nothing. No rent deduction. No recognition of cost-of-living spikes. When your landlord raises the rent, your life tightens—but the law doesn't notice. Meanwhile, someone with a paid-off mortgage might be kicked off Medicaid due to home value increases. Rewarding ownership shouldn't become institutional punishment. But this law doesn't just punish renters—it punishes living.

Disabled Community Left on the Sidelines
One of the few empathetic touches in the original design was nutrition education tied to SNAP. That's gone, along with the funding for community outreach on diabetes, healthy shopping, and cooking. People with disabilities, who often face higher food costs, lose a lifeline. ABLE accounts still exist—but they're unsupported. Deductions exist—but complexity dilutes access. This isn't about removing inefficiency—it's about removing means.

The Quiet Sabotage of Hardship Relief
What families need isn't a snapshot of equity—they need a safety net that stretches through crisis. But this policy checks eligibility during times of illness, unemployment, or caregiving. It doesn't register temporary strain—it checks permanence. Miss a deadline? Insurance for your kid drops. Income spikes? No child tax credit. Home equity goes up

again? No long-term care. Life's volatility becomes your disqualification.

Structural Inequity, Not Incidental Outcomes
When no one funds outreach to educate communities about changing thresholds—when no one staffs translation lines—equity cracks. Data from affluent areas shows marginal decline in benefit uptake. In communities already struggling, that decline becomes structural absence. Marginal service reductions become permanent losses. That's how access is robbed quietly, legitimately, and unfairly.

The Myth of Neutrality—Policy by Proxy
The law suggests neutral mechanics, but the outcomes aren't accidental. They're the arithmetic of policy design. "We don't discriminate—but only those who hit these numbers get filtered." Except the numbers themselves are stacked. They rely on constant W2 income, single-digit medical expenses, home ownership within state caps, and flawless paperwork. That's not neutral—it's normative. It normalizes the assumption that families look like you, live like you, and file like you.

Equity Requires Flexibility—This Law Offers None
When we face wildfire, flood, recession, recession, or pandemic, we expect adaptive policy. Use tax credits to stoke rebuilding. Teach nutrition classes when food access collapses. Allow graduated benefits when income falters. This law locks everything in place. Festivals end. Fires kill. Houses burn. Grocery lines lengthen. But the law doesn't care. It doesn't adjust. It enforces. That's equity denial.

Access Isn't a Perk—It's a Path

Universities, skills centers, job retraining—they close quietly. When state funding hinges on graduate education performance, schools tailor for high-performing, standardized applicants. That squeezes out nontraditional students—working parents, displaced workers, late-career students—people whose promise isn't linear. Access isn't a perk. It's a pipeline. And the law dismantles pipeline, piece by piece.

Demographics of Exclusion

Who's excluded? Mixed-status families, gig workers, renters, rural residents, disabled individuals, victims of climate or economic upheaval. That's not a fringe—it's half the population. Every policy line may seem limited, but combined, they create concentric circles of exclusion that radiate outward—by degree, not accident.

Moral Solvency Demands More

Equity isn't a checkbox. It's an iterative commitment, built through engagement, funding, oversight, and humility. This law sets none of that. Instead, it raises the walls so only the methodologically perfect can enter. It says: we'll support you—but only if you look exactly like our spreadsheet. And if you don't? Then good luck.

Chapter 34: Legislative Game Plan

Forget the optics—they banked this bill on timing, complexity, and legal entrenchment. From day one, the architects choreographed a legislative coup masquerading as policy reform. They weaponized deadlines, sunsets, and

forensic phrasing to insulate this package from real scrutiny—
and make reversals near-impossible.

Timeline as Tactic

Major provisions launch January 1, 2026—for everything
from tax cuts to work requirements. Medicaid and SNAP
escalations pause into 2027–2028. Student-loan rules align
with the next academic year. That stagger isn't accidental—it's
smoke and mirrors. The public sees immediate relief—or
doom—but never connects the dots when gradual pain sets
in. It dissipates political backlash. By the time the wall-to-wall
impact hits, elections have passed; awareness has cooled.

Sunsets as Shields

Insert a five-year timer under "Trump accounts" or senior
deductions, and suddenly Congress can claim fiscal
responsibility. But there's no obligation to revisit or report—
just quietly let it expire. Most Americans will never realize that
"senior tax breaks" vanished—again—for the same reason
they never noticed they returned. Defunding by
disappearance: effective, insidious, invisible.

Deadlines Without Resources

The law screams "agencies must do this by X date" but
whispers "no money, no staff, no tech, no help." Want SNAP
work requirements? USDA must implement regardless of
platform readiness. Considering inflation? Not without a
court battle. Want disaster exemptions? Too bad. If an agency
delays, states or individuals sue. It costs them nothing to
derail—and agencies lose public trust, face litigation, or lose
roles. Because for lawmakers, literalism beats competence
every time.

Bond Requirement: Suits without Access

Want to challenge implementation? Better hope you can afford a bond first. It's political insulation—no injunctions unless bond's posted. That keeps litigation off the radar, protects agencies from class-action rulings, and downgrades public accountability. Lawsuits won't die on merits—they'll die on cost. It's legislative game theory.

Attack Surface by Complexity

The bill isn't one clean statute. It's dozens of overlapping chapters: SNAP, tax, immigration, student loans, energy, Medicaid. Each adjusted by thresholds, phase-outs, caps, conditions, waivers, sunsets. That complexity isn't incompetence—it's camouflage. Where one clause would trigger national uproar, this labyrinth ensures no single group sees the full picture until it's irreversible. Dissatisfaction emerges piecemeal—too late for political reversal.

Precision Language as Pure Weapon

The architects chose every word with strategic intent: "shall not," "no discretion," "frozen," "notwithstanding," "unless reauthorised." It's language meant not to govern, but to nail it in place. No wiggle room, no reinterpretation, no executive mitigation. That's not statute—it's technical artillery. It ensures that even a sympathetic administration must return for Congress just to raise a comma.

Federal vs State: Litigation Strategy

By giving state attorneys general standing to sue over enforcement or non-enforcement, they cloaked oversight in local control. Want stricter SNAP? AG steps in. Want leniency on asylum? AG resists. That brutalizes cross-state cohesion—encouraging enforcement extremes and forcing agencies to either follow or face inter-state lawsuits. Federal authority gains magnitude; litigation becomes the enforcement mechanism.

Agency Subordination to Courts
It shifts power from bureaucratic expertise to judicial interpretation. Agencies lose policy-making tools. Courts gain primacy in procedural minutiae. Enforcement isn't policy—it's litigation risks. So staff default to caution, inertia, or textualism. That ensures national commitment, regardless of partisan change.

This Is Precedent, Not Policy
This bill isn't a textbook example—it's an engineering run. The intent was clear and explicit: make it hard—legally, politically, administratively—to unwind. They didn't just design policy—they designed permanence. And they did it quietly, under the radar of public debate.

Why It Wins Politically
Laypeople hear "tax relief for families," "clip waste in government," or "protect energy independence." Headlines capture endless bullet points—no nuance, no cumulative consequences. Further debate? Too late. By 2024, public memory is short, focus moved. But policy rolls out on schedule. Opponents are always playing catch-up.

The Real Risk: Entrenched Error
Code written like this takes on moral and legal inertia. Contractors, lawyers, agencies, think-tanks, lobbyists—all become enmeshed. Repealing it means unraveling multilateral obligations, renegotiating contracts, revoking incentives.

You're not undoing a poorly performing policy—you're defusing a multi-decade architecture.

The Wake-Up Call
If you glance at policy without reading the legal wiring, you'll miss the plan. This chapter exists to expose the design, spotlight the stakes, and call for vigilance. The question isn't "should we adjust it?" The question is "how do you reform a fortress?"

Because once game theory trumps policy substance in legislation, democracy loses its teeth. We can't just "vote it away." We need structural, coordinated action: litigation capacity, public awareness, oversight coalitions, and constitutional leverage. Otherwise? The law just runs on its own momentum—and we keep reacting, never reversing.

That's the legislative game plan: hide the sword in the statute, build resistance into deadlines, weaponize complexity, mute agency power, entrench inequality, and let the machinery hum. The good news: nothing is impossible to change. The bad news? Right now, that machinery hums louder than any public will to dismantle it.

Chapter 35: Restricted Agency Flexibility

This law does not tolerate improvisation. It doesn't allow agencies to adjust, to delay, or to deviate—no matter the crisis, no matter the stakes. It codifies rigidity under the banner of oversight and hands Congress a legislative whip that lashes the executive branch into submission. Discretion? Gone. Waivers?

Eliminated. Emergencies? Irrelevant. The agency doesn't respond to conditions. It responds to statute. Period.

Every word of this bill is designed to pin agencies down. The bureaucratic flexibility that once let regulators pause enforcement, soften rules, or adapt midstream is surgically removed. Provisions are locked to fixed implementation dates. Language prohibits reinterpretation. Clauses like "shall not be suspended," "shall apply regardless of circumstance," and "without exception" replace what once allowed administrative judgment. This isn't about clarity. It's about control—control from legislators who know exactly what they're doing: stripping away executive agency power while pretending it's about efficiency.

Before this, when disasters hit—a hurricane, pandemic, recession—agencies acted. USDA issued waivers for food stamp recertifications. CMS delayed Medicaid redeterminations. The IRS postponed deadlines. FEMA coordinated across health and housing systems. They weren't overstepping; they were maintaining function. This law declares such responses a violation of statute. Congress, having passed the law, now sits back and dares the executive to blink. If an agency delays enforcement, even to stop mass harm, it risks court intervention or statutory breach. The result is not faster government. It's paralyzed government.

There is no waiver language. There is no catch-all clause allowing secretaries to delay rule implementation in the public interest. Even rules that rely on future funding or state collaboration must move forward—on time, as written. The absurdity is immediate. A state might be unable to process new Medicaid work requirements by the deadline, but the agency cannot pause enforcement. Families lose coverage. Courts may step in, but only after the damage is done.

This rigidity also strips institutional knowledge from the process. Federal departments are staffed by career professionals with decades of domain-specific insight. Their entire function—historically—was to balance the law's intent against on-the-ground conditions. That function has been abolished. The text now rules them. They cannot soften abrupt policy shifts. They cannot provide phased rollouts. They cannot issue delay memos or grant compliance extensions. The law has tied their hands behind their backs and nailed their feet to the floor.

And if they try to innovate? Try to interpret? Try to act as thinking agents in a complex world? State attorneys general—armed with new legal standing—will sue them into submission. Even if agencies win in court, the chilling effect is achieved. Staff do not act because the risk of acting exceeds the mandate to serve. That is how a modern regulatory regime dies—not with a dramatic firing or defunding, but through quiet suffocation by legal constraints.

All of this is done under the guise of democratic supremacy. Legislators point to the bill and say, "We are the people's voice." But stripping flexibility from executive agencies doesn't empower voters—it cages professionals. It removes the very system that once allowed government to evolve, react, and course-correct.

And the implications are everywhere. In SNAP, this rigidity means a single missed paycheck—due to system failure, employer error, or illness—can't be administratively forgiven. In Medicaid, it means someone dropped during a technical issue cannot be re-enrolled with retroactive eligibility unless another statute intervenes. In tax policy, it means deadlines can't be shifted even when forms change or IT systems fail. In immigration, it means an asylum rule applies retroactively, regardless of legal status at the time of filing. Every clause is a trap. Every sentence is a weapon against discretion.

There is no emergency escape. No backdoor flexibility. No implied authority. The bill doesn't just remove elasticity; it forbids its return. Legislative supremacy is the architecture, and every agency is a tenant with no keys to its own office.

This isn't what most Americans think when they hear "rule of law." They imagine fairness, clarity, predictability. What they get is brittle enforcement, unable to bend in the face of reality. A grandmother loses her SNAP because the agency must process her form by a fixed date, even though the office lost power. A single mother misses a Medicaid redetermination deadline and loses coverage for her child because there's no extension process allowed. A state trying to implement energy subsidies can't delay rollout despite lacking contractors or materials. This is what rigidity looks like—not efficiency, but failure by inflexibility.

The cruelty is procedural. The outcome is engineered. The system is failing exactly as designed.

And this is the final insult: when it collapses, no one will blame the law. They'll blame the agencies. The frontline worker. The overburdened office. The "lazy bureaucrat." Not the text that forbade discretion. Not the legislators who wrote it that way on purpose. They'll call it government failure—because it is. And yet, it's government failure mandated by law.

The bill didn't just define policy. It redefined what agencies are allowed to be: no longer facilitators, no longer responsive arms of democratic governance, but enforcers of code, incapable of interpretation, unable to protect the vulnerable, and legally prohibited from adapting—even when it's life or death. That's not oversight. That's sabotage. Codified, enforced, and permanent.

Chapter 36: Legal Bond Barrier

The premise is simple: you can still sue the federal government—if you can afford to. The bill introduces a bond requirement for legal challenges against federal agencies, a calculated chokehold on the ability of individuals, nonprofits, or small entities to hold power to account. They've quietly replaced the principle of access to justice with a price tag. Justice isn't denied outright. It's auctioned.

This isn't about preventing frivolous lawsuits. That argument's a fig leaf. Federal courts already have tools to dismiss baseless claims. What this bond requirement actually does is deter anyone without deep pockets from even stepping into the courtroom. You want to challenge an immigration denial? Pay up first. Think the IRS wrongly calculated your tax credit under the new law? Post a bond equal to the potential liability. Want to delay a harmful policy's rollout while the courts consider your argument? That'll cost you, up front, in cash.

These bonds don't refund just because you were right. You post them to proceed, not to win. The threshold to impose them is deliberately vague: courts may require them "where there is a substantial impact on administrative operations."

That could mean anything. And in a system where agencies are already stripped of discretion, courts become the gatekeepers—and now they get to tax entry.

This is a direct assault on legal equity. Wealthy entities—corporations, state governments, politically connected plaintiffs—can lawyer up, pay the bond, and pursue litigation. Everyone else? Sit down, shut up, and take your medicine. Your child lost Medicaid because of a system error? File a complaint if you must, but if you want to stop it through the courts, hope your GoFundMe catches fire. Otherwise, you're done before you begin.

Nonprofits and advocacy groups are especially boxed out. They don't sit on capital reserves. They depend on grants, donors, and time-sensitive campaigns. For them, even a small bond requirement is enough to shelve litigation. Strategic public interest lawsuits—those long, slow-burning challenges to unjust policy—become too expensive to initiate. The law turns civil rights litigation into a luxury good. Even class-action pathways are obstructed, as bond rules can apply per plaintiff or by total potential liability. One miscalculation and your case bankrupts your organization before the opening brief.

The real genius of the bond requirement is its chilling effect. Most potential plaintiffs won't even try. Once word spreads that filing a federal suit means risking your savings or your organization's future, the fear sets in. Not because of bad law—but because of high stakes. This fear isn't irrational—it's learned. It's strategic. And it's exactly what the authors of the bill intended.

They knew what they were doing. They saw how litigation overturned policy before—healthcare mandates, immigration orders, benefit denials. And they decided, "Let's make the court the bottleneck." They couldn't remove judicial review outright, so they monetized it. The power to sue is still on the books. It just costs more than most Americans can pay.

This isn't a bug in the system. It is the system. The law erects procedural fortresses that only the well-financed can storm. The rest are left pounding on a locked door with empty fists. This bond requirement doesn't protect government function—it protects government failure. It ensures that no matter how sloppy, cruel, or incompetent a policy may be, it can roll forward uninterrupted unless the challenge is backed by cash.

And when that happens, when the courts are only accessible to those who can buy the ticket, the law ceases to be a neutral arbiter. It becomes a privatized tool. You don't win on merit—you win on affordability. The bond system doesn't just distort justice. It auctions it off.

People will say, "Well, we need to keep the courts from being flooded." That's nonsense. Courts dismiss frivolous cases all the time. They have clerks, standards, filters. What they don't need is a velvet rope guarded by a price list. The bond doesn't make things fair. It makes them exclusive. It treats civic participation like a transaction.

This is the same strategy used in voter ID laws, in tax code opacity, in means-tested programs with impossible paperwork. Raise the cost of participation—time, money, or complexity—and watch the unwanted drop out. This bond requirement is no different. It cloaks its cruelty in administrative language, knowing that most people will never realize they've been pushed out of the justice system until it's too late.

And let's be clear: this will not affect government contractors, corporate plaintiffs, or high-net-worth individuals. They'll still sue. They'll still delay enforcement. They'll still shape policy through litigation. What changes is who can't. What changes is who's removed from the fight before it begins. The government has just decided that litigation—a foundational check on its power—should be a pay-to-play service.

It's not framed that way, of course. They'll say the bonds are a safeguard, a formality, a filter. They'll say most people won't be affected. They'll insist it's to prevent disruption. What they won't say is the quiet part: that this kills small-scale resistance before it starts.

This chapter of the bill is one of the most dangerous, not because it affects benefits or taxes, but because it rewrites the rules for who gets to challenge anything. It doesn't change what's legal—it changes who can afford to prove what's illegal. And in doing so, it pulls one of the final threads of accountability from a system already frayed to the core.

Chapter 37: Longevity by Legal Rigidity

This law wasn't built to last because it's good. It was built to last because it's hard to kill. Every clause, every phrase, every structural hook is a legislative deadbolt—designed not to govern better, but to govern longer. Permanence by design, not merit. This is the difference between policy that survives on function and policy that survives by trapdoor. What we're looking at here is legal architecture designed for political immortality.

The strategy is straightforward: bury the mechanics in hard-coded language that resists reinterpretation. You won't find soft phrases like "subject to review" or "unless determined necessary." No agency flexibility. No secretarial override. No standard of reasonableness. Instead, this bill uses concrete statutory commands that force future governments to comply—whether they agree or not. It doesn't just legislate policy. It locks it behind legal vaults.

Take implementation dates. They're not tied to funding or administrative readiness. They're fixed, absolute, and court-enforceable. That means even a future Congress must pass new legislation just to delay execution. And passing new legislation means political capital, filibuster math, and a willing White House. Good luck with that trifecta. Even bad ideas stay locked in because the mechanism to unbolt them is deliberately cumbersome.

This is how modern laws shield themselves from repeal: not with popularity, but with process. Strip waiver authority. Remove catch-all clauses. Nail down effective dates. Then throw in a few fiscal triggers that require offsets for repeal. If you want to unwind it, you now have to identify funding, draft replacement rules, and defend them in court. It's not protection—it's a cage. And Congress built it for itself.

They've also engineered interdependence. This bill doesn't operate as one big machine. It's a thousand gears moving in sync. Change one, and you disrupt five others. A tweak to SNAP work requirements? Now you're looking at Medicaid eligibility misalignment. Adjust a tax threshold? It collapses phase-in tables for dependent care. Everything is cross-referenced. This is legislative entanglement. And it guarantees that reformers will hesitate, not because they're cowards, but because the math is impossible.

Then there's the regulatory language. The bill uses nested definitions that force agencies into narrow interpretations. You can't redefine "work activity" because it's now a statutory term with locked criteria. You can't broaden "dependent care" unless you amend ten separate references. The statute interprets itself, preemptively. And in doing so, it locks out human judgment.

The brilliance of this rigidity is that it outlasts its authors. No matter who wins the next election, the bill remains operational. Agencies can't ignore it. Courts must uphold it. New secretaries can't waive it. It doesn't bend—it enforces. It doesn't expire—it resets. It becomes self-renewing, a regulatory automaton that survives regardless of public sentiment or administrative leadership.

And when the public starts to feel the pain—benefit cliffs, healthcare drop-offs, tax confusion—the response isn't legislative clarity. It's legislative gaslighting. "Well, we need a new bill." "Well, that's the agency's problem." "Well, if you don't like it, elect someone else." By the time a functional coalition comes together to repeal any part of it, the damage is permanent, and the interests too entrenched.

Even the sunset clauses are a scam. On paper, they imply review. In practice, they create political hostage scenarios. Let a provision expire and someone somewhere gets hurt. That turns every sunset into a cliff Congress doesn't want to go near. So provisions are extended automatically—or worse, locked in under the pretense of avoiding disruption. Nothing is evaluated. Everything persists.

Legal rigidity here isn't accidental. It's insurance. It's how lawmakers inoculate themselves against the volatility of democracy. They know laws can be unpopular. They know elections can swing. So they wrote permanence into the scaffolding, like engineers designing a bridge meant to survive fire, flood, and sabotage—not because it's beautiful, but because it's too expensive to replace.

And the longer it stays, the more bureaucratic infrastructure gets built around it. Training manuals, IT systems, litigation protocols, state budgets—all designed to comply with a law no one fully understands anymore. At a certain point, even if you repeal the statute, the machinery stays. The institutional muscle memory is too deep. So now you're not just fighting a law—you're fighting the entire government's way of working. That's what longevity by rigidity really means.

This is how bad policy becomes untouchable. Not because it works, not because people love it, but because it's too hard to dismantle. And that's by design. Every time someone tries to change it, they run into cost estimates, delay threats, agency pushback, procedural hurdles, and political risk. The law endures because the alternatives are exhausted before they begin.

So here we are, watching an architecture that prioritizes durability over justice, complexity over clarity, rigidity over responsiveness. It's not broken—it's frozen. And unless someone is willing to burn political capital, sink time, risk litigation, and battle a hundred nested clauses, it stays that way.

This wasn't governance. It was legislative entrenchment. And it worked.

Chapter 38: Everyday Impact Snapshot

Policy doesn't live in CBO scores or legislative summaries. It lives in kitchens, doctor's offices, job sites, and daycares. This bill, with its spreadsheet precision and legal fortifications, hits real people in the face every single day—and none of them will recognize the language that did it. They'll just feel the absence. Of time, of coverage, of help. This wasn't a policy written for visibility. It was built to be felt invisibly, like a trapdoor you don't know you're standing on until it opens.

Start with a working-class family in Ohio. Both parents work inconsistent schedules—retail and food service. Their three kids qualify them for the expanded child tax credit, but one bad filing year puts them over the phase-out threshold. Their youngest starts daycare, and suddenly they lose dependent care eligibility too. When their shifts fluctuate, they miss the new 80-hour-a-month requirement for SNAP by a single week. The system doesn't ask why. It just terminates benefits. Now they're not eating better. They're eating less.

Move to a retiree in Florida. She's 72, owns her home, and has limited savings. The new Medicaid asset test counts more of her equity, pushing her out of long-term care eligibility. She doesn't know this until her third home aide visit gets denied. The phone lines are backed up, the county office understaffed. Her daughter, already covering groceries, must now find $1,800 a month for private care. All because the law quietly decided that owning your house means you don't need help.

Jump to a single gig worker in Arizona. He drives rideshare, picks up freelance design jobs, and occasionally tutors. His income swings wildly—$3,000 one month, $700 the next. None of the tax credit phase-ins account for this variability. He doesn't qualify for the new tip and overtime exemptions either—those are capped. He earns too much to get help, too little to save, and too inconsistently to plan. He files his taxes late, loses deductions, and discovers his marketplace insurance premium jumped. His only mistake? Having the kind of job Congress doesn't understand.

In Michigan, a mixed-status household gets their SNAP cut in half. Why? Because the undocumented cousin's income is now factored in. She doesn't qualify for benefits herself, but her earnings subtract from everyone else's allotment. It's not a glitch. It's law. That household must now choose between paying rent or eating three meals. They do both—by not paying the gas bill.

Meanwhile, a nonprofit in rural Mississippi that used to offer diabetes education has shuttered. SNAP-Ed is defunded. Their community partner, a local grocer who hosted free healthy cooking classes, ends the program. The store sees declining foot traffic. Local seniors stop learning what foods won't spike their insulin. Medication adherence drops. Hospitalizations rise. No one tracks this. There's no provision for it in the bill. But it's real.

Then there's the community college counselor in Nevada trying to help students navigate financial aid. The new cap on graduate loans means fewer students even consider postgrad work. The expanded 529 flexibility doesn't help students without families who saved early. And the student loan matching for employer payments? It's lovely—if you have a white-collar job that offers it. The rest are buried in debt, told to be patient, and denied forgiveness. Because what matters now is cost-neutral compliance, not upward mobility.

Every example plays out quietly. There's no mass protest. No front-page coverage. The damage isn't dramatic—it's granular. A copay here. A benefit clawback there. A deduction phased out. A reapplication denied. A timeline missed. A waiver not available. That's how erosion works—not with explosions, but with pressure, over time, until the structure gives out.

The most devastating thing about this bill is how normal the fallout will look. Not like a collapse, but like a pattern of daily failures. That's how people will describe it: "I just can't catch a break." "I'm doing everything right, and it's still not enough." "I used to qualify, but I guess I don't anymore." They'll think the problem is them. That's the genius of complexity. It makes systemic cruelty feel like personal failure.

Even the wins are booby-trapped. A family receives a $1,000 Trump Account for their newborn. They can't contribute more, but the account isn't indexed to inflation. By the time the kid's 18, it's barely enough for a semester of community college. But Congress gets to point at it and say they did something. Meanwhile, tax credits designed to help the middle class phase out before most of them ever claim them. The law pretends to reward responsibility, then penalizes the exact behavior it preaches.

And here's the kicker: people won't be mad at the law. They'll be mad at their landlord, their boss, their social worker, their HR rep. They'll yell at IRS hold music, at case managers, at their kids' school nurse. Because they'll never connect their daily unraveling to a bill signed three years earlier. That's the design. Policy becomes pain without memory.

This isn't just bad governance. It's a masterclass in hiding consequences. The suffering is distributed, atomized, and backloaded. There's no moment of reckoning—just an accumulation of strain that becomes the new normal. That's how people give up. Not all at once, but piece by piece.

This is what legislative impact actually looks like. It's not abstract. It's not ideological. It's the missing inhaler refill, the shorter grocery list, the canceled dental appointment, the postponed FAFSA, the layoff from a clean energy job that never came back. It's every broken promise, rebranded as tough love, reform, or efficiency.

They call it responsible policy. In practice, it's structural abandonment. And nobody gets to opt out.

Chapter 39: Winners, Losers, and Trade-Offs

Every bill picks winners. This one just does it with more dishonesty than most. The rhetoric paints it as a balancing act—help here, trim there, no one too hurt, everyone gets something. But the ledger tells a different story. The winners are precise, wealthy, and politically aligned. The losers are diffuse, marginal, and expendable. And the trade-offs aren't real—they're sacrifices, dressed in technocratic language to blunt the cruelty.

Start with the obvious winners: high-income earners in low-tax states. By locking in the standard deduction and keeping SALT capped, the bill rewards taxpayers who never itemize. It's a gift to upper-middle-class households in Texas or Florida while punishing those in states like New York or California. But since that's already been spun as a fight over "blue state bailouts," no one blinks. Wealthier Americans also benefit from the deduction for car loan interest—so long as it's not a luxury car. Translation: they get to write off their SUV, just not their Porsche. Hardly populist.

Next are fossil fuel producers. The bill restores full depreciation schedules, expands intangible drilling cost deductions, and pulls back clean energy incentives. That's not market neutrality—it's legacy protection. Oil and gas get handouts. Clean tech gets a knife in the ribs. Investors win. Innovators lose. The supposed "energy balance" is just old money reclaiming dominance with legislative cover.

Large employers come out ahead, too. The employer-paid student loan matching sounds generous, but it benefits firms that already offer robust benefit packages—tech companies, finance, healthcare giants. The working-class employer? They can't afford it. Their workers don't get matched payments. They just keep drowning in debt. But the headlines don't differentiate, so it all sounds like progress.

And then there are the losers. Gig workers, renters, blended families, aging caregivers, rural communities, part-time students—anyone whose life doesn't fit a narrow mold of financial predictability gets penalized. Variability becomes a flaw. Flexibility becomes noncompliance. The system doesn't accommodate—it excludes. Because it wasn't written for them.

States with fragile safety nets lose, too. With reduced cost-sharing and rising administrative requirements, they're expected to do more with less. Their punishment for having lower tax bases and stretched agencies is harsher oversight, fewer waivers, and bigger penalties. The federal government offloads its workload onto them, then blames them for failing. It's austerity disguised as accountability.

Families with mixed immigration status lose quietly but comprehensively. Their ineligible members' incomes count against benefits. Their access to programs tightens. Their paperwork burden doubles. And when things go wrong, there's no help desk—just denials. The law doesn't even have to say "no." It just builds a system where the answer is always "not quite."

Seniors looking for long-term care lose subtlety. They're told to spend down their homes to qualify for Medicaid, just as property values peak. Their children are left navigating a maze of eligibility thresholds, estate recovery clauses, and escalating care costs. What was once a modest protection becomes a barrier to survival. The same law that gifts auto deductions to the affluent tells grandma her house is too nice for nursing care.

Now to the trade-offs, the so-called compromises. The Trump Accounts—$1,000 baby bonds for kids born over four years—are symbolic scraps. They look generous until you realize inflation devours their value before the kid hits grade school. Medicaid pilot programs must be budget-neutral from day one. That's not reform. That's policy theater. No program addressing generational poverty breaks even immediately. But the bill doesn't care—it rewards the appearance of cost control, not its reality.

Child tax credits are expanded, but structured to phase out exactly where many middle-class families live. Have three kids and two incomes? Good luck keeping the full benefit. Working full-time but don't have custody? No help for you either. The formula rewards consistency, not complexity. The law sees your life as a line graph. If your income zigzags, you lose.

Even the work requirements come with pre-loaded consequences. They're pitched as incentives but function as tripwires. Miss the 80-hour mark in one month, and benefits shut off. No grace period. No catch-up clause. Just automatic removal. The logic? If you wanted help, you'd work harder. Never mind the scheduling conflicts, childcare gaps, transportation failures, or health issues. The law doesn't accommodate life. It punishes deviation.

And the final insult: everyone's told this is "bipartisan." Because a few moderate concessions are baked in—like senior deductions that expire or token flexibility in benefit cliffs—it's sold as a balanced meal. But it's not balanced. It's calculated. Every provision was placed to protect the law, not the people. Every giveaway was matched by a clawback buried three pages deeper. This isn't compromise. It's containment. And the net effect is inequality with paperwork.

This bill didn't fail by accident. It didn't miscalculate. It made deliberate choices. It chose to invest in capital, not care. In compliance, not flexibility. In enforcement, not empathy. The winners got more tools. The losers got more hoops. And everyone else? They got the burden of pretending it's their fault.

So, yes—there are winners. But they were chosen. And there are losers. And they were discarded. And the trade-offs? They were written to look fair while gutting the margins. That's not policy. That's legislative sleight-of-hand. And too many people are falling for it.

Chapter 40: Equity and Access Concerns

Equity is the most abused word in modern policy, and this law is no exception. It parades equity in the preamble, references it in press releases, and sprinkles it across talking points like seasoning. But when you strip out the performance, what's left is a system engineered to entrench exclusion. It doesn't expand access. It curates it. It doesn't correct systemic disadvantage. It makes it invisible, by building eligibility criteria so opaque that no one knows they've been disqualified until they're already off the rolls.

Start with the basics. Equity, properly applied, means accounting for different starting points and removing barriers that punish circumstances beyond someone's control. This bill does the opposite. It assumes uniform lives, smooth income, consistent documentation, centralized infrastructure, and uninterrupted digital access. Anything outside that model is punished by design. If your hours fluctuate, if your paperwork gets delayed, if your address changes mid-month—you're out. Not because you failed, but because you didn't match the fantasy profile written into statute.

And while the law doesn't explicitly name who gets excluded, it doesn't have to. Its criteria do it for you. Live in a mixed-status household? The income of the ineligible members still counts, reducing your food benefits. Need Medicaid while caring for a parent? Too much home equity means you're now too wealthy to qualify, even though you're functionally broke. Try to finish your degree part-time while working? Your tuition credits evaporate. You're not prohibited. You're just erased from the math.

The structure punishes those most likely to fall through cracks: renters who move often and miss re-certifications, gig workers whose income disqualifies them in good months but fails to support them in bad ones, seniors who can't navigate portal logins, disabled applicants who depend on outdated documentation, low-literacy households with no translation support. These aren't edge cases. They're predictable realities.

And the law anticipates them not to fix them, but to filter them out.

What's passed off as efficiency is often just strategic attrition. By requiring quarterly income reporting, the law ensures churn. By limiting waiver flexibility, it guarantees noncompliance. By centralizing verification processes with no corresponding funding, it manufactures delay. And every drop-off, every missed re-enrollment, every quiet exit is counted as budget savings—not as lost access, not as unmet need, just as one fewer headache to track. This is how inequity is repackaged as administrative success.

Even the "inclusive" pieces are built with cliff effects. The child tax credit expands—until you hit a dollar over the phase-out threshold. The Trump Accounts are available—until the calendar flips to 2030. The auto loan deduction helps drivers—until the IRS deems your car too nice. The law's few carrots are paired with tripwire conditions that most people don't even know they've triggered until the benefits vanish.

Digital access only worsens the divide. Online-only recertification systems with rigid submission windows don't serve the public—they serve the bureaucracy. The law presumes every household has a scanner, stable internet, legal literacy, and time. Meanwhile, community organizations that once helped bridge that gap are defunded or drowned in new compliance rules. Translation services? Minimal. Outreach? Scrapped. You can't access what you can't understand, and this bill is written to be misunderstood.

And let's not ignore geography. States already stretched thin will fail first. Rural offices with skeleton staff will collapse under reporting demands. Urban offices facing high volume will bottleneck. States that made past policy mistakes now face reduced funding shares. Those most in need of support are those least capable of maintaining compliance under these conditions. The law says, "we've standardized the rules." What it means is, "we've ignored your capacity."

This is not a failure of intention. It's the intention itself. Policymakers understood full well that tightening eligibility, increasing reporting, and removing administrative discretion would hit marginalized communities hardest. But they counted on those communities having the least political leverage. It's not accidental. It's targeted apathy.

True equity requires flexibility. It demands pathways that acknowledge complexity and systems that support navigation. This law gives neither. It assumes competence, consistency, and capacity from populations that have been systemically denied all three. It confuses gatekeeping with governance. It replaces service with surveillance. And then it dares to call that "fair."

What we're left with is a system that only looks equitable on paper—because paper doesn't bleed. It doesn't show the eviction notices that followed a missed credit. It doesn't record the skipped medication after a Medicaid drop. It doesn't tally the hours lost on hold, the miles driven to appeal, or the dignity eroded one denied claim at a time. But it sure does calculate savings. And that's the point.

This bill isn't blind to equity. It's hostile to it. Not in rhetoric, but in reality. It builds a path forward, then places traps along the way, daring people to stumble. And when they do, the law doesn't help them up. It walks past, satisfied the system worked exactly as intended. That's not reform. That's exclusion in legislative drag.

Made in the USA
Las Vegas, NV
11 July 2025

24802904R00095